A

GUIDE

TO

SPIRITUAL

GROWTH

A Guide To Spiritual Growth

Union Hill Publishing
200 Union Hill Drive, Suite 200
Birmingham, AL 35209

www.richardesimmons3.org

ISBN 978-1-939358-42-4

12345678910

Printed in the United States of America

CONTENTS

Why are We Here? 3

Salvation Is A Gift 6

Responding To The Gospel Part I 9

Responding To The Gospel Part II 13

Responding To The Gospel Part III 16

Adoption 19

Knowing Christ 21

Seeking God 23

What Is The Bible? 25

Listening To God Part I 28

Listening To God Part II 31

Spending Time With God 34

Talking With God Part I 36

Talking With God Part II 39

Praying For God's Protection 41

How To Talk To God Part I 44

How To Talk To God Part II 47

How To Talk To God Part III 49

Praying For A Changed Life Part I 52

Praying For A Changed Life Part II 55

Praying For A Changed Life Part III 58

The Triune God 62

The Power Of
The Holy Spirit Part I 65

The Power Of
The Holy Spirit Part II 68

The Power Of
The Holy Spirit Part III 70

Building A Strong
Foundation 73

The Storms Of Life Part I 76

The Storms Of Life Part II 79

The Storms Of Life Part III 82

The Storms Of Life Part IV 84

God's Light 87

The Promises Of God 90

Seeking God's Guidance 93

A Love Of The Truth 95

One Of Life's Most
Significant Principles 98

The Value Of Wisdom 101

The Significance Of Biblical
Prophesy 103

Being Emotionally Healthy 106

God's Objective For The
Christian Life Part I 109

God's Objective For The
Christian Life Part II 112

INTRODUCTION

This guide is designed to assist you in growing spiritually and moving towards spiritual maturity. The first five lessons aim to help you fully understand the message of salvation and how we are to respond to it properly. In one sense, it serves as a review of teaching you may have already received, but these first five lessons are foundational and must be fully understood in order to grow spiritually.

The first lesson examines the issue of purpose and why God has put us here. In lesson two, we consider probably the most critical theological issues in the Bible. Finally, in lessons three through five, we examine the necessary response for a person to become a true, authentic Christian.

Then, in lesson six through forty, this guide contains foundational teachings that must be understood and put into practice in order to grow spiritually and to know Christ at a deep level.

I suggest reading one lesson per day. After completing each lesson, I suggest you go through it three more times, one each day. This will truly allow you to grasp the foundations of our faith.

—Richard E. Simmons III

WHY ARE WE HERE?

Several years ago, *USA Today* published the results of a survey that had been conducted with a fairly large group of people. They were asked this: If you could ask God one question, and He would give you the answer, what would that question be?

The number one response in the survey was: "I would ask God; why am I here? What is the reason for my existence?"

This should not surprise us, because this is a question people throughout the ages have asked, going all the way back to the early Greek philosophers. The Greeks believed in a concept called the "logos." It literally means "word" but has an important secondary meaning; "reason" or "reason for life." It is also where we get the word "logic." The Greek philosophers were in search for the logos, the reason for life. They believed when you found it, you would be whole and complete as a person. The problem is, they never could agree on the logos. They could never come up with a unified answer.

It appears that all people are trying to find purpose and meaning in this earthly life. Yet, we must realize purpose and meaning imply design. For instance, your smart phone clearly has a purpose. It is not just a piece of plastic. It did not come into existence by itself or by accident. It clearly had a designer. Purpose implies design, and, of course, in order to have design, you must have a designer. When you consider a human being, his or her purpose is not as apparent and clear. For this reason, we must look to God, our Designer, to discover the answer to the questions:

What was I designed to do?

What is the purpose of my life?

In the Bible we are given two clues about our design. The first clue is found in the book of Genesis.

> *"So, God created man in His own image..."* Genesis 1:27

> *"For in the image of God, He made man."* Genesis 9:6

This means we possess a number of God's characteristics that none of His other creatures possess. For instance, we have a personality and emotions because He has a personality and emotions. He gave us the ability to think, reason, and be creative because He thinks, reasons, and creates. In fact, if we were not relational beings, there would be no such thing as loneliness. Furthermore, the Bible is quite clear that we, as human beings, love others because God is a God of love. We are told that we have the ability to love because God first loved us. (I John 4:19)

There is a second clue about our design that helps us truly understand our reason for being here. A number of verses in the Bible, from both the Old and New Testaments, reveal this clue.

> Isaiah 43:21–*"The people whom I formed for myself will declare My glory."*

> Colossians 1:16–*"For by Him all things were created, both in the heavens and on earth, visible and invisible, whether thrones, dominions, rulers, or authorities, all things have been created through Him and for Him."*

> I Corinthians 8:6–*"...and we exist for Him, one Lord Jesus Christ."*

> I Corinthians 1:9–*"God is faithful through whom you have been called into fellowship with Jesus Christ our Lord."*

God made us for Himself so that we would live in a meaningful love relationship with Him. It is the same reason parents choose to bring children into the world: we anticipate a lifelong relationship with them. The Bible describes this relationship as such: He is our heavenly Father, and we are to be His children. All of this explains Augustine's famous words: "God, you have created us for Yourself, and our hearts will not find rest until they rest in Thee."

The Apostle Paul tells us in Colossians 2:10, *"In Him, (Christ) we are made complete."* Through this relationship with Christ, we fulfill the purpose of our earthly existence and become complete as people. Conversely, to live without Him is to live without purpose and be incomplete, always searching for something to make us feel whole.

NOTES:

SALVATION IS A GIFT

Sometimes I believe one of the most difficult spiritual truths Christians have trouble grasping is that you cannot earn your way into heaven. In other words, you do not gain entrance into heaven by following the law, what the Bible calls "works of the law."

I think at times we find that this belief comes naturally because this is how normal life works. Whether it is work, sports, or academics, generally you have to earn what you receive. You work hard and you reap from your efforts.

However, when it comes to getting into heaven you are not capable of getting in on your efforts, because you are a sinner.

> *"For all have sinned and fall short of the glory of God."*–Romans 3:23

It is because of our sin that we are separated from God.

> Isaiah 59:2–*"But your iniquities have separated you from your God; your sins have hidden his face from you, so that he will not hear."*

What we then learn is that our salvation is a gift of God.

> Romans 6:23–*"For the wages (consequence) of sin is eternal death, but God's free gift is eternal life through Jesus Christ our Lord."*

> II Corinthians 9:15–*"Thanks be to God for His indescribable gift!"*

God's gift to us is an act of grace. Grace is defined as "God's undeserved favor." Paul explains this clearly in Ephesians 2:8,9:

> *"For it is by grace you have been saved, through faith—and this is not from yourselves, it is the gift of God—not by works, so that no one can boast."*

Then, in Romans 3:24, Paul says:

> *"...we are justified as a gift by his grace."*

There is a very good parable that helps us understand grace.

A PARABLE:

There was a very bright, ambitious young man who upon graduating from business school moved to Silicon Valley to begin his career. He was very creative and quite the entrepreneur. At the age of 28 he left his place of employment to start his own technology firm. His new company grew and flourished and a week before his 35th birthday, he took the company public. At the end of the first day of trading the stock, this young man was a billionaire.

Later that night, he experienced a real sadness in that he had no one special to share in this great moment. He appeared to have everything except meaningful relationships. All he had ever done was work. He was married to his business. He realized how lonely he was and that he yearned for a wife and family.

Across town there was a lovely young woman who had worked her way through college, taking out student loans to pay her way. She was an accomplished musician, graduating with honors as a music major. After college, she fulfilled her passion by teaching music to underserved youth.

As fate would have it, this lovely young woman and the man in our story, the billionaire, are introduced to one another by a mutual friend at a symphony event. They immediately connect and, over time, fall in love, and eventually get married.

The moment they become husband and wife; all his fortune becomes hers. All his riches come to her because she said yes to him and entered into the covenant relationship of marriage.

Think about it. One person has done everything in order to create this wealth. The spouse gets married and receives this wealth by grace.

This is a picture of God's grace. We are like the music teacher. As she receives her husband's monetary wealth, we receive the wealth of God's grace. We did nothing. Jesus did everything at the cross. When we are united with Him, everything that Christ has done on the cross is true for us. We are credited with His righteousness.

So, God's salvation is a gift and all we must do is receive the gift. And Jesus is the gift. By faith we receive Him into our hearts.

> John 1:12– *"But as many as received Him, to them He gave the right to become children of God."*

> Colossian's 2:6– *"As you have received Christ Jesus the Lord, so walk with Him."*

I think this lesson can be summarized in Paul's words in Galatians 2:16:

> *"Yet we know that a person is made right with God by faith in Jesus Christ, not by obeying God's law. And we have believed in Christ Jesus, so that we might be made right with God because of our faith in Christ, not because we have obeyed the law. For no one will ever be made right with God by obeying the law."*

NOTES:

RESPONDING TO THE GOSPEL
PART I

I n Lesson 2, we spoke of receiving Christ into your life. However, there is another word used often in scripture that we must understand. It is the word "believe". You will see that these two words are connected. You are probably familiar with John 3:16:

> *"For God so loved the world, that He gave His only Son, so that everyone who believes in Him will not perish but have eternal life."*

And John 6:47:

> *"Truly, truly, I say to you, the one who believes has eternal life."*

These verses both make it clear that you have to believe in order to have eternal life. In English the word "believe" is a friendly word. The big question is what does it really mean to believe in Him. Every time you see the word "believe" in the New Testament, it comes from the Greek word *pisteúō*, which means so much more than just believing something in my head. It means "believe in, to entrust, to rely on, to cling to."

Imagine you wake up one morning, you feel sick and know something is terribly wrong with you. You go to the doctor who then sends you to the hospital where they run a battery of tests. You are then told by the attending physician that what he has discovered is both good news and bad news.

The bad news is that you have a rare form of cancer, and if it goes untreated you will be dead within six months. The good news is that it is very treatable, and with proper chemotherapy there is a 100% recovery rate.

You breathe a sigh of relief because you believe what he has told you is true. But you need to do more than believe it in your head. True belief is completely entrusting your life into the doctor's care. It is completely relying on him and being willing to do whatever he instructs you to do. This is *pisteúō*. This is what it means to believe.

Another way of looking at this is to remember what we are talking about when we consider what it means to become a Christian. We are talking about entering into a relationship with Christ.

However, there is another relationship in this life. It is a holy relationship, and you have to enter into it as well. It is called Holy Matrimony.

I know some people find it odd that in four different places in the Gospels,

Jesus is referred to as the bridegroom. In John 3:29 John the Baptist says:

> *"He who has the bride is the groom; but the friend of the groom, who stands and listens to him, rejoices greatly because of the groom's voice. So, this joy of mine has been made full."*

In Matthew 9:15:

> *"And Jesus said to them, "The attendants of the groom cannot mourn as long as the groom is with them, can they? But the days will come when the groom is taken away from them, and then they will fast."*

In Mark 2:19:

> *"And Jesus said to them, "While the groom is with them, the attendants of the groom cannot fast, can they? As long as they have the groom with them, they cannot fast."*

In Luke 5:34:

> *"And Jesus said to them, "You cannot make the attendants of the groom fast while the groom is with them, can you?"*

Jesus refers to Himself as the Bridegroom, which explains why the church, the people of God, have always been referred to as the "bride of Christ."

The language used here—that of a bride and bridegroom—is the language describing a wedding where two people come together to be united in a holy ceremony. A wedding is one of the most significant events in life. We are entering into a whole new life.

Jesus uses the terms bride and bridegroom to demonstrate how we enter into a relationship with Him—a life-changing relationship. The next time you go to a wedding with a traditional ceremony, listen to the opening words:

"Dearly beloved, we are gathered together here in the sight of God and these witnesses, to join together this man and woman in holy matrimony, which is an honorable estate, instituted of God, signifying the mystical union that exists between Christ and His church."

The church has always recognized that marriage signifies and is a picture of what takes place between Christ and His people. Both relationships have to be entered into.

A COVENANT RELATIONSHIP

When people consider marriage, they will at some point count the cost of entering into this relationship. To many it means they are giving up being single, their independence, and their ability to make unilateral decisions. Everything they own becomes part of their spouse's possessions. It is a significant commitment, which is what God intended.

Marriage paints an accurate picture of what we must consider before entering a relationship with Christ. Many falsely believe they can become Christians with no real commitment on their part. They think they can serve Christ on their own terms. Jesus makes it clear we must completely entrust our life to Him if we want to be a true believer.

The next time you go to a wedding, pay close attention to the exchanging of vows. In essence, the bride and groom are giving themselves completely to each other. This is what must happen if you are to become a Christian. But know this, Jesus has already given Himself to us at the cross.

> Galatians 1:3,4 – *"Grace to you and peace from God the Father and our Lord Jesus Christ, who gave Himself for our sins so that He might rescue us from this present evil age, according to the will of our God and Father."*

> Ephesians 5:2 – *"and walk in the way of love, just as Christ loved us and gave himself up for us as a fragrant offering and sacrifice to God."*

> Ephesians 5:25 – *"Husbands, love your wives, just as Christ also loved the church and gave Himself up for her,"*

> Titus 2:13,14 – *"looking for the blessed hope and the appearing of the glory of our great God and Savior, Christ Jesus, who gave Himself for us to redeem us from every lawless deed, and to purify for Himself a people for His own possession, eager for good deeds.*

These verses all speak of Jesus giving Himself to us when He voluntarily laid down His life at the cross.

So, picture this: Jesus is the bridegroom, and He is saying to each of us, "I have given Myself up for you, I have laid down My life for you. Will you receive Me, and will you completely entrust your life into My care? Will you surrender your heart? Ultimately, will you believe?"

NOTES:

RESPONDING TO THE GOSPEL
PART II

I think one of the best ways to fully understand how we should respond to the Gospel is found in probably the most well-known parable in the Bible. It involves a father and his two sons. Though we learn a great deal from the lives of both sons, I want to focus on the first son, the one that many call the Prodigal Son. We get a wonderful picture of how this son, who represents us and our rebellion, gets back into right relationship with his father (who represents God).

The parable is found in Luke 15:11-24. I will share the basic story and make comments along the way.

A man had two sons and the younger son approached him and asked for the share of the estate that would one day be due him. Surprisingly, the father said yes. A few days later, the young son gathered all his wealth and possessions and traveled to a distant country. He then proceeded to squander his wealth on reckless and wild living.

This young son left his home looking for a better life, and he seemed to think he knew where to find it. He left with a real sense of freedom. I am sure he had the same attitude so many young people have today—they are bullet-proof and are going out to conquer the world.

Most significantly, he wanted to get away from his father's presence. The young son wanted his father's money and financial support but did not really want anything to do with his father. This is so true of us. We want the blessings of God, but we just don't want God in our lives.

This young son did not want to live under his father's authority; he wanted the freedom to live however he chose to live. This, of course, is a picture of our sinful heart.

As the parable continues, the young son squandered everything he had and ended up with a job feeding pigs. No one was giving him anything. He was truly humbled, and I am sure he realized that he was not, in fact, bullet-proof. His pursuit of the good life had broken down; and because his money was gone, no one around him seemed to really care.

We are told in the text that he finally came to his senses and recognized how lost he was. I am sure he also realized the cold hard fact that the world was not devoted to his happiness or well-being. He also recognized his true condition—he was dead and lost.

The parable goes on to say that the son finally recognized his need for his father. He was now able to see clearly and realized there was someone who loved him and cared for him. He knew his father at least would give him a job. However, in order to return to his father, he saw the need to do two essential things. Pay close attention to these two things because they are necessary for us to get into right relationship with God.

In the balance of this lesson, I will share the first component of his response and in the next lesson I will lay out the second.

First, the son recognized that he was a sinner and needed to confess his sins. The text says, "I will get up and go to my father, and will say to him, 'Father, I have sinned against heaven and in your sight; I am no longer worthy to be called your son.'" The son recognized his need for his father's forgiveness, and he acknowledged his sin and asked the father's forgiveness.

This is the heart of salvation, the forgiveness of our sin. I often have to remind people that good people do not go to heaven, but it is forgiven people that go to heaven.

In Luke 1:77, Zacharias speaks of *"...giving the people the knowledge of salvation by the forgiveness of their sins."* In Colossians 1:14, Paul speaks of God's beloved Son *"in whom we have redemption, the forgiveness of sins."* And in Acts 10:43, Peter says that through Christ's name, *"everyone who believes in Him receives forgiveness of his sins."*

What we ultimately need to do is to acknowledge we are sinners and are looking to Christ to be our Savior.

NOTES:

RESPONDING TO THE GOSPEL
PART III

The Prodigal Son recognized that he was sinful, and he needed his father's forgiveness.

The second realization the son had is that in order to get back into right relationship with his father, he had to leave his wayward lifestyle and return home on his father's terms. He could not go back on his own terms. The son was leaving his old life for a new one.

Unfortunately, what happens in the lives of so many people is they want to be a Christian but only on their own terms. A true believer is one who is willing to surrender their will to Christ and follow Him. It means turning our heart away from self and turning toward God. This is what the Bible calls repentance. It is to surrender.

We are by nature sinful human beings, wanting to live for self and be ruled by self. This is why we are called to repent and surrender.

We do not hear many people talk about or teach on repentance today. However, you would be stunned at the number of times it is mentioned in the Bible. Over the years, I have met with many men who are searching spiritually. At a certain point I have them read eight or nine verses that speak of repentance and ask them in advance, before reading, "How important is repentance in becoming a Christian?" Most of them do not consider it to be important. We then read these verses:

II Peter 3:9–*"The Lord is not slow about His promise, as some count slowness, but is patient toward you, not willing for any to perish, but for all to come to repentance."*

Matthew 4:17–*(Jesus was returning from 40 days in the wilderness and was beginning His ministry.)* *"From that time Jesus began to preach and say, "Repent, for the kingdom of heaven is at hand."*

Luke 3:3–*"And he came into all the region around the Jordan, preaching a baptism of repentance for the forgiveness of sins;"*

Luke 13:3–*"No, I tell you, but unless you repent, you will all likewise perish."*

Luke 13:5–*"No, I tell you, but unless you repent, you will all likewise perish."*

Luke 24:45-47–*"Then He opened their minds to understand the Scriptures, and He said to them, "So it is written, that the Christ would suffer and rise from the dead on the third day, and that repentance for forgiveness of sins would be proclaimed in His name to all the nations, beginning from Jerusalem."*

Acts 3:19–*"Therefore, repent and return, so that your sins may be wiped away, in order that times of refreshing may come from the presence of the Lord;"*

Acts 17:30-31–*So having overlooked the times of ignorance, God is now proclaiming to mankind that all people everywhere are to repent, because He has set a day on which He will judge the world in righteousness through a Man whom He has appointed, having furnished proof to all people by raising Him from the dead."*

After reading these verses, I again ask the question, "How important is repentance in becoming a Christian?" The response I always get at this point is: "It seems to be essential." The dilemma comes when people realize that they believe in God and Jesus and want their sins forgiven, but they often are not willing to repent and surrender.

Repentance is an issue of the heart. It becomes a battle over who is going to rule over our heart. The Apostle Paul nailed our dilemma when he said in Romans 2:5:

> *"But because of your stubbornness and unrepentant heart you are storing up wrath for yourself on the day of wrath and revelation of the righteous judgment of God."*

C. S. Lewis says that what made atheism so attractive to him was that he could gratify his wishes and live however he pleased. This was also true of the young son in the parable.

However, when Lewis came to believe in God and recognized that Jesus was the Son of God who had died for his sins on the cross, it was only logical for him to surrender. It is like choosing to serve in the army of a powerful king. You do not negotiate with the king and tell him what you are willing to do. You bend your knee to him and serve him with your life.

In his book, *Mere Christianity*, Lewis says,

"Now what was the sort of 'hole' man had got himself into? He had tried to set up on his own, to behave as if he belonged to himself. In other words, fallen man is not simply an imperfect creature who needs improvement:

he is a rebel who must lay down his arms. Laying down your arms, surrendering, saying you are sorry, realizing that you have been on the wrong track and getting ready to start life over again, from the ground floor—that is the only way out of our 'hole.' This process of surrender—this movement full speed astern—is what Christian's call repentance."

Lewis is saying that the arrogance of man insists, "I belong to myself, and I will run the show." The Christian humbles himself and declares, "I surrender and follow You."

This is what it means to have Christ as your Lord. In order to be a true Christian and enter into a relationship with Christ, you must look to Jesus as your Savior and Lord.

NOTES:

ADOPTION

I n lesson one, we looked at the reason for human existence and we answered the question, "Why did God put me here?" We considered the two clues that God has given us to answer this question and concluded that He put us here to live in relationship with Him.

However, there are all different types of relationships in life. Yet, God has made it clear what type of relationship He desires with us in John 1:12.

> *"But as many as received Him (into their lives), to them He gave the right to become children of God..."*

So many people falsely believe that all human beings are children of God, but you do not see that taught anywhere in the Bible. Before we receive Christ, we are human beings of great value because we are created in the image of God. I also might add that we are of such great value because He loves us. But we are not in relationship with Him. He is not our heavenly Father. He is the God of the universe and one day He will be our judge.

However, when we receive Him into our lives, we become His children by way of adoption. He adopts us into His family, and He becomes our heavenly Father.

> Romans 8:15–*"The Spirit you received does not make you slaves, so that you live in fear again; rather, the Spirit you received brought about your adoption to sonship. And by him we cry, 'Abba, Father.'"*

> Galatians 3:26–*"So, in Christ Jesus, you are all children of God through faith."*

> Galatians 4:4-7–*"But when the set time had fully come, God sent His Son, born of a woman, born under the law, to redeem those under the law, that we might receive adoption to sonship. Because you are his sons, God sent the Spirit of His Son into our hearts, the Spirit who calls out, "Abba, Father." So, you are no longer a slave, but God's child; and since you are his child, God has made you also an heir."*

> I John 3:1–*"See what great love the Father has lavished on us, that we should be called children of God! And that is what we are! The reason the world does not know us is that it did not know Him."*

Ultimately, God wants to adopt us into His family, and we become one of

His many children. As a Christian, we are a child of God.

Every parent that desires to have children does so by anticipating a love relationship with their children that has the potential for great joy and closeness. This is why we are told in Psalm 149:4 that He takes great pleasure in us. In fact, He delights in us and desires to bless us as any parent desires for their children. What a great privilege we have in that we can bring great delight and pleasure to the God of the universe who is our Heavenly Father.

Jesus tells us that as earthly parents, our love for our children is flawed because we are sinners. Yet, our Heavenly Father's love for us is perfect.

As sinful parents nevertheless, there is one desire we have for our children, that overrides all other desires. We yearn and desire the best for them. Is God, our Heavenly Father, any different when it comes to us and our lives?

Yet, God faces an obstacle, us, and our wills. We so easily believe that we know what is best for our lives.

As one man put it, there are two states of being, submission to God and His will, or the refusal to submit to anything except one's own selfish will. The big question becomes, whose will are we going to submit to?

NOTES:

KNOWING CHRIST

A number of years ago, I heard a speaker begin his talk with this question, "What is your definition of a Christian?" I think he may have surprised everyone in the audience with his answer. He said, "A Christian is someone who has a personal relationship with Jesus Christ." You do not see this definition in the Bible, but there are a number of verses that infer this.

When you develop a personal relationship with someone, you begin to get to know them. The Bible speaks often of knowing God and knowing Christ.

In the Old Testament, we read King David's last words to Solomon, his son:

> *"As for you my son Solomon know the God of your father and serve Him with a whole heart and a willing mind."*—I Chronicles 28:9

> *"Let not a wiser man boast of his wisdom and let the mighty man boast of his might, let not a rich man boast of his riches, but let him who boasts boast of this, that he understands and knows Me, that I am the Lord."*—Jeremiah 9:23, 24

> *"So, let's learn, let's press on to know the Lord. His appearance is as sure as the dawn; And He will come to us like the rain, As the spring rain waters the earth."* — Hosea 6:3

> *"I will give them a heart to know Me, for I am the Lord, and they will be my people and I will be their God."* — Jeremiah 24:7

Then, in the New Testament, there are some powerful verses on knowing Christ.

> *"Yes, everything else is worthless when compared with the infinite value of knowing Christ Jesus my Lord."*—Philippians 3:8

> *"I want to know Christ and experience the power of His Resurrection."*—Philippians 3:10

> *"And we know that the Son of God has come and has given us understanding so that we may know Him who is true..."*—I John 5:20

> *"This is the way of eternal life, that they may know You, the only true God and Jesus Christ whom you have sent."*—John 17:3

Finally, there are a number of verses that indicate you are not a Christian if you do not know Christ.

> *"God will deal out retributions to those who do not know God."*
> —II Thessalonians 2:8

> *"Formerly, when you did not know God, you were slaves to those which by nature are not God's."*— Galatians 4:8

> *Finally, in the famous Sermon of the Mount, Jesus talks about the Judgement Day and reveals that on that day, many will claim to be Christians. They will tell of all the good works they did in Jesus's name. They will then hear these shocking words declared by Christ, "I never knew you, depart from Me."*—Matthew 7:21-23

Think about what the Apostle Paul said back in Philippians 3:8, that everything in life is worthless when you compare it with the incredible value of knowing Christ. The reason is that this is what we were made to do, and this is what makes us complete.

NOTES:

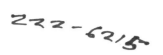

SEEKING GOD

I n order to grow and develop, relationships require time spent together. It involves communication, where we speak and they listen, and then they speak, and we listen. This is how we get to know someone.

Spiritually, we speak to God through prayer, He speaks to us through the Bible. We will talk about this further in future lessons. However, in order for any relationship to move forward, time has got to be allocated for this to happen. Spiritually, God does not barge into our lives each day, He invites us to seek Him. In fact, each day He desires to spend time with us, but He gives us the responsibility to seek Him.

Something I noticed recently is how the Scripture speaks of God's blessings and favor to those who seek Him.

> *"The young lions do lack and suffer hunger; but they who seek the Lord shall not be in want of any good thing."* —Psalm 34:10

> *"The hand of the Lord is favorably disposed to all those who seek Him."* —Ezra 8:22

> *"The Lord is good to those whose hope is in Him, to the one who seeks Him.* —Lamentations 3:25

> *"And without faith it is impossible to please Him, for he who comes to God must believe He exists and He rewards those who earnestly seek Him.* —Hebrews 11:6

> *"They who seek the Lord understand all things."* Proverbs 28:5

God has promised us that if we will seriously seek Him, that we will find Him.

> *"And you will seek Me and find Me when you search for Me with all your heart."* —Jeremiah 29:13

> *And then, Jesus tells us: "Ask and it shall be given to you, seek and you shall find, knock and it shall be opened to you."* —Matthew 7:7

Our responsibility is to seek God with the intent of knowing Him, so that He will be a living reality in each of our lives. Over time, you will begin to know Him personally as He reveals more of Himself to you. Then as you continue to pursue Him, you will begin to really love Him. If you think about it, you cannot really love someone deeply, until you know them.

NOTES:

WHAT IS THE BIBLE?

Human speech that can be clearly understood, documented through the written word, is the model that God has chosen to reveal Himself to us down through the ages.

In fact, in the Old Testament, we are told how God's written words came into being. In the opening sentences of Jeremiah's first chapter, we are told that these words are the words of Jeremiah (Jeremiah 1:1), and then in verse 2, we are told that the Word of the Lord came to him. As John Stott says:

> *"So, Scripture is neither the Word of God only nor the words of men only, but the Word of God through the words of men...This is the double authorship of scripture to which we need to hold fast."*

As Peter himself described it, he said:

> *"God's word is not an act of human will, but men moved by the Holy Spirit spoke from God."* (II Peter 1:21)

So, Biblical truth is inspired truth...but it is also eyewitness truth. You see this in both the Old and the New Testaments. As Peter, making reference to the Transfiguration, says, *"We were eyewitnesses of his majesty."* And the apostles who authored and approved the New Testament books were eyewitnesses of the Risen Christ. In fact, that was required to be an apostle, and, as John Stott says:

> "...this eyewitness principle lies behind all scripture, for God raised up witnesses to record and interpret what he was doing in Israel."

The first two thirds of the Bible is the Hebrew Bible which the church inherited from the Jews. It is called the Old Testament. It is divided into three sections. They call these three sections the law, the prophets, and the writings, and each of these sections covers one of three successive periods in history.

In the early books of the Old Testament, it had been recognized from ancient times that if God's revelation is to be preserved, it had to be written down. For instance, in Exodus 17:14, after Israel led by Joshua had defeated one of their enemies, and where God had clearly intervened to help them, God said to Moses,

> *"Write this on a scroll as something to be remembered."*

In Deuteronomy 31:24, God speaks to Moses and tells him to write in a book the "words of my law." God then says to Isaiah (Isaiah 30:8):

> *"Now go write it on a tablet before them, and inscribe it on a scroll that it may serve in the time to come as a witness forever."*

It becomes clear that God wanted certain historical events and spiritual truth written down and documented for the benefit of future generations. That would include each of us.

Then, Jesus enters the world and you read about His life in the first four books (Matthew, Mark, Luke, and John) of what is called the New Testament. But, who wrote the New Testament?

If you look at Luke 24:48, John 15:27, and Acts 1:8, you see that Jesus makes it very clear that His apostles were to be designated witnesses and spokesmen out in the world after He was gone.

They were special men, and they had a special appointment, and you will notice in the four gospels that the twelve are referred to as His disciples. The word disciple means "a learner." In other words, what you had were these twelve men, and they were learning. They were being trained and equipped. They had been fishermen, tax collectors, and common lay people, and He was pouring His life into them, teaching them and instructing them. Later, Jesus appoints them as apostles, and then, of course, after Jesus' death, Judas kills himself and is replaced by Matthias. And, you have Saul of Tarsus who also is appointed as an apostle. He becomes the apostle Paul and is clearly recognized by all the other apostles as being one of them. They approved it.

And this is what's so important to know: the word "apostle" means something completely different from "disciple." An "apostle" is a messenger. An emissary, a representative. They started out as students, as disciples, and then, He gave them the authority to be his representatives, His apostles out in the world. And He gave them a unique authority in the church. And this authority, this "apostleship," was not passed down. The apostles became agents of God's revelation, documenting what would become the Christian source of faith and life—The New Testament. And having been commissioned by Jesus, one of their primary assignments was clearly seen in John 14:26 and John 16:13-14. These are Jesus' words; He says:

> *"But the Helper, the Holy Spirit, whom the Father will send in My name. He will teach you all things and bring to your remembrance all that I have said to you."* (John 14:26)

> *"But when He, the Spirit of truth comes, He will guide you into all truth; for He will not speak on His own initiative, but whatever He*

hears, He will speak; and He will disclose to you what is to come."

"He will glorify Me, for he will take of Mine and will disclose it to you." (John 16:13,14)

This is where we get our understanding of the inspiration of Scripture, where God himself is involved with the process of leading and guiding the apostles in their writings. Peter reminds us that the words of Scripture were not acts of human will, "but men moved by the Holy Spirit spoke from God." Therefore, in early church history, you see this pervasive recognition that the written words of the apostles were given full authority.

NOTES:

LISTENING TO GOD

PART I

A real relationship involves listening and talking between two people. But how do you listen to God? It is quite clear that God reveals Himself to us, primarily through the Bible.

We are told this about God's written Word.

Hebrews 4:12–*"For the Word of God is alive and active. Sharper than any double-edged sword, it penetrates even to dividing soul and spirit, joints and marrow; it judges the thoughts and attitudes of the heart."*

I Thessalonians 2:13–*"And we also thank God continually because, when you received the Word of God, which you heard from us, you accepted it not as a human word, but as it actually is, the Word of God, which is indeed at work in you who believe."*

The Bible is like no other written piece of literature you will ever encounter. It's alive and active, it is like a sword that pierces our souls. As we read His Word, it performs a work in our lives.

As you read the Old Testament, there is a critical issue that exists between God and His people. It impacted their well-being and was essential to spiritual growth.

Deuteronomy 13:4–*"You shall follow the LORD your God and fear Him; and you shall keep His commandments, listen to His voice, serve Him, and cling to Him."*

Isaiah 50:4–*"The Lord God has given Me the tongue of disciples, so that I may know how to sustain the weary one with a word. He awakens Me morning by morning; He awakens my ear to listen as a disciple."*

Jeremiah 42:5, 6–*Then they said to Jeremiah, "May the LORD be a true and faithful witness against us if we do not act in accordance with the whole message with which the LORD your God will send you to us. Whether it is pleasant or unpleasant, we will listen to the voice of the LORD our God to whom we are sending you, so that it may go well for us when we listen to the voice of the LORD our God." Clearly, God's desire is for us to listen to His voice.*

It is crucial for us to realize that one of the most important traits of the God of the Bible is He is not silent and is not hidden. He reveals Himself to us—He speaks into our lives. He tells us.

1. As your God, I desire for you to listen to My voice.

2. This is the commitment He makes to us.

> Psalm 32:8–*"I will instruct you and teach you in the way which you should go; I will counsel you with My eye upon you."*

3. In this verse God is telling us something more specific. He is saying not only do I desire to speak To you, I also want to give counsel. Think about why people go to counsel? Generally, we need guidance because we have a need in our lives. Our Heavenly Father wants to offer counsel and guidance which will lead to our well-being.

4. Another verse that addresses our great need to listen to God's voice is:

> Isaiah 48:17–*"This is what the Lord says -your Redeemer, the Holy One of Israel: I am the Lord your God who teaches you what is best for you, who directs you in the way you should go."*

We should greatly desire to read God's Word because the all-wise God of the universe desires to teach us what is best for us.

So, the challenge we face is when we go to read our Bible, we should see it more than an act of duty, but rather an opportunity to hear God's voice. That He might speak to me, give me counsel, and teach me what is best for me.

This is why before you even open your Bible, you should pray:

"Lord, I am here to seek You, I am here to listen to Your voice."

"I love Samuel's prayer in I Samuel 3:9, *"Speak Lord, Your servant is listening."*

This is the heart of the Christian life because we are speaking of communion with God. It is a major component in how we come to know God.

NOTES:

LISTENING TO GOD
PART II

I believe one of the highest priorities in life is to seek to listen to God's voice in the Bible. There is an incident described in the Scriptures that might not seem significant, but it reveals a vital truth about our priorities.

> Luke 10:38-42–*As Jesus and his disciples were on their way, he came to a village where a woman named Martha opened her home to him. She had a sister called Mary, who sat at the Lord's feet listening to what He said. But Martha was distracted by all the preparations that had to be made. She came to him and asked, Lord, don't you care that my sister has left me to do the work by myself? Tell her to help me! Martha, Martha, the Lord answered, You are worried and upset about many things, but few things are needed—or indeed only one. Mary has chosen what is better, and it will not be taken away from her.*

Notice the words that are used to describe Martha, "distracted, worried, and upset." These are accurate words to describe modern people. Does that ever describe your life?

Look at Jesus' response to Martha. He is not telling her that her preparations in the kitchen are wrong or immoral. This is a priority issue. He is telling Martha what really matters most in life.

What Jesus is revealing through this incident is that we as humans get so busy and distracted by so many issues that don't really matter. Often, they are trivial issues and activities.

I know a gentleman who is a real Greek scholar, and this is the way he translated if from the actual Greek text: "Martha, you have let yourself be taken with many cares. Mary is focused on the one important thing in life."

So, what was Mary doing? Go back and look at verse 39. It says she "sat at the Lord's feet listening to what He said."

I believe Jesus wants us to know that listening to Him is the most important priority in life. There is another incident that is quite significant that emphasizes this same point:

> Matthew 17:1-8–*After six days Jesus took with him Peter, James, and John he brother of James, and led them up a high mountain by themselves. There he was transfigured before them. His face shone like the sun, and his clothes became as white as the light. Just then*

there appeared before them Moses and Elijah, talking with Jesus. Peter said to Jesus, "Lord, it is good for us to be here. If you wish, I will put up three shelters—one for you, one for Moses and one for Elijah." While he was still speaking, a bright cloud covered them, and a voice from the cloud said, "This is my Son, whom I love; with him I am well pleased. Listen to him!" When the disciples heard this, they fell face-down to the ground, terrified. But Jesus came and touched them. "Get up," he said. "Don't be afraid." When they looked up, they saw no one except Jesus.

Jesus has taken Peter, James, and John, three men who will be some of the most important leaders of the early church, and He has taken them high upon the mountain. This bright cloud covers them, and they hear this voice. The voice of God the Father. You would think He might have a great deal to say to these future leaders. His only instruction to them is to listen to Jesus. Again, I believe this should be the most important priority in life.

There is a great illustration from Stephen Covey to help us to better understand our priorities. He uses it to help us understand our activities by dividing them into four quadrants.

1 Important	2 Not Important
3 Urgent	4 Not Urgent

Quadrant 1 is the important, urgent activities in life. Almost everyone understands this. If your largest client leaves you a message that he needs to speak with you as soon as possible, you call him immediately.

Quadrant 2 is not important, but urgent activities in life. You see an example of this in Luke 10. Martha's preparations were urgent to her, but, as Jesus points out, it was not vitally important.

Quadrant 3 are those activities that are not important and not urgent. Watching television would generally fall in this category.

Quadrant 4 Covey believes that people who really flourish are those who have the discipline and the will to focus so much of their time on the important but not the urgent activities in life. This would include planning, continuing education, and reading. I am convinced the most important activity in life is nurturing your soul by listening to God. And though it is the most important activity in life, it is not urgent.

NOTES:

SPENDING TIME WITH GOD

To hear God's voice in the Bible, you have to be willing to give Him regular time to speak to you. You have to be willing to give Him part of your day. If we do not, then by default we are indirectly saying to Him, "I don't have time for You, there are other issues in my life that are more important than my relationship with You."

It is also important to realize that since God does not speak to us audibly, but quietly to our hearts, we need a time of solitude, we need quietness.

Think about the opening words of the 23rd Psalm:

> *"The LORD is my shepherd, I will not be in need. He lets me lie down in green pastures; He leads me beside quiet waters."*

Notice that He makes me to lie down in green pastures, He leads me beside quiet waters. Why quiet waters? Could this be for spiritual reasons?

In Psalm 46:10, in the New International version it says: "Be still and know that I am God." Yet, in the New American Standard version, "cease striving and know that I am God." Literally, it means to relax and let go.

This reminds me of Martha back in Luke 10 in lesson 7, where we read of Martha who was "distracted, busy, and worried." In essence, I think Jesus was trying to tell Martha, "cease striving," be still, be quiet, listen to what I have to say to you.

So, we all need a quiet place where we can be still.

It is important to pray before you start your daily reading. Consider some of these prayers that came right out of the Bible:

> Psalm 119:18– *"Open my eyes, that I may behold wonderful things from Your Law."*

> Psalm 32:8– Ask God to *"instruct you and teach you in the way which you should go; I will advise you with My eye upon you."*

> Psalm 43:3– *"...send out your light and your truth, let them lead me."*

> Psalm 25:5– *"Lead me in your truths and teach me, for You are the God of my salvation, for You I wait all day."*

> Psalm 119:28– *"Strengthen me according to Your word."*

> 1 Samuel 3:9– *"Speak Lord for your servant is listening."*

Colossians 3:16–*"Let the word of Christ richly dwell within me."*

A natural question to ask is, where do you start reading? How much do you read in one sitting? There is no right answer. However, what is important is not the quantity of what you read but the quality of your time with God.

I suggest you start reading a chapter a day from the New Testament starting with Matthew. I also suggest a reading from the Old Testament, like a Psalm or Proverb. Keep a record of what you read each day and record meaningful verses that you read. You may even want to memorize some of these verses. This is why I believe you need a notebook of some kind.

Finally, it is important to not read too much in one sitting. Read slowly and lightly. Let the words speak to you. You might even read it prayerfully where you pray over something you have read.

I encourage you to be patient with the process. It takes a while to become accustomed to what you are doing, but over time it will impact your life and perspective, and it will become an indispensable part of your daily life. Most significantly, you will be getting to know and understand your heavenly Father.

NOTES:

TALKING WITH GOD

PART I

O ur focus has been on our relationship with Christ. A relationship involves speaking and listening. In lessons 10-13 we considered the importance of listening to God's voice in the Bible. We now want to focus on talking to God and developing a prayer life.

It is interesting how many people view prayer. Some see it as a way you get what you want in life. Also, it is something you do when you are in trouble or are struggling with worry or fear. But is that God's intent for prayer?

Look at what Jesus says in Luke 18:1:

"Now He was telling them a parable to show that at all times they ought to pray and not become discouraged,"

We will look at the parable in a later lesson, but He makes it clear here that we should pray at all times. In other words, we should pray often.

Why is prayer important? Philip Yancey says, "The main purpose of prayer is not to make life easier, nor to gain magical powers, but to know God."

After studying the prayers found in all the Psalms, Yancey says, "I learned from the Psalms to converse with God as I would converse with my employer, my friend, my wife—in short to treat God as a person in every sense of the word. I had seen prayer as a kind of duty, not as a safe outlet for whatever I was thinking or feeling. The prayers of the Psalmist freed me to go deeper."

Mother Teresa said, "prayer is simply talking to God. He speaks to us, and we listen. We speak to Him, He listens. A two-way process: speaking and listening."

One of the most striking features of prayer is that it is the ultimate act of faith. In Hebrews 11:27 we are told:

"By faith Moses left Egypt, not fearing the wrath of the King, and he endured as seeing and believing in God who is unseen."

When we pray, we are praying to our God who we cannot see, but the reason we pray is because we believe that He hears us. This is faith.

Consider what scripture says about prayer, though it may not use the word prayer.

Psalm 116:1, 2–*"I love the Lord, because He hears my voice and my pleas. Because He has inclined His ear to me, therefore I will call upon*

Him as long as I live."

Psalm 25:1–*"To You, Lord, I lift up my soul."*

Psalm 145:18–*"The Lord is near to all who call on Him, To all who call on Him in truth."*

Psalm 62:8–*"Trust in Him at all times, you people; Pour out your hearts before Him; God is a refuge for us."*

Jeremiah 33:3–*"Call to Me and I will answer you, and I will tell you great and mighty things, which you do not know."*

Matthew 7:7-11–*"Ask, and it will be given to you; seek, and you will find; knock, and it will be opened to you For everyone who asks receives, and the one who seeks finds, and to the one who knocks it will be opened. Or what person is there among you who, when his son asks for a loaf of bread, will give him a stone? Or if he asks for a fish, he will not give him a snake, will he? So if you, despite being evil, know how to give good gifts to your children, how much more will your Father who is in heaven give good things to those who ask Him!"*

Notice the language.

"Call out to Him"
"Pour out your heart to Him"
"Lift up your soul to Him"
"Ask from Me."

God desires for us to have an authentic relationship with Him, where we speak to Him as we would speak to another person. However, I might add, we are speaking to our Heavenly Father.

NOTES:

TALKING WITH GOD

PART II

There are two issues related to prayer that we need to be aware of. The first involves our heart attitude as we approach God. In Psalm 10:17 we see these words:

> *"O Lord, You have heard the desire of the humble, You will strengthen their heart, you will incline Your ear."*

Then In II Chronicles 7:14 we read:

> *"If My people who are called by my name will humble themselves and pray and seek my face and turn from their wicked ways, then I will hear from heaven, will forgive their sin and will heal their land."*

The attitude of our hearts that we bring before God is crucial. Theologian Ole Hallesby said the word "helplessness" is the single best word to describe the heart attitude we bring before God.

This is particularly difficult for men who grow up and are taught to be self-reliant and self-sufficient. If we are not careful, we can seal off the attitude of our hearts that is most desirable to God.

This is why Philip Yancey says, "the heart of prayer is a declaration of our dependence on God."

Think about King David, a fearless and mighty warrior, who had great courage. Look at the attitude of his heart in this prayer in Psalm 30:10:

> *"Hear O Lord, and be gracious to me, O Lord, be my helper."*

The second issue has to do with the motive behind our prayers. In James 4:3 we read:

> *"When you ask, you do not receive because you ask with wrong motives so that you may spend what you desire on your pleasures."*

I believe we need to give serious consideration over what we pray about, and not be frivolous over what we pray.

Whenever a difficult situation arises in your life it is natural to ask God to remove it. However, what if His intent is to use it in your life to mold and refine your character? What if He intends to use it for your good?

This is what Paul learned in II Corinthians 12:7-9:

"Because of the extraordinary greatness of the revelations, for this reason, to keep me from exalting myself, there was given to me a thorn in the flesh, a messenger of Satan to torment me—to keep me from exalting myself! Concerning this I pleaded with the Lord three times that it might leave me. And He has said to me, "My grace is sufficient for you, for power is perfected in weakness." Most gladly, therefore, I will rather boast about my weaknesses, so that the power of Christ may dwell in me.

God was seeking to keep Paul from exalting himself and being conceited. He also wanted Paul to experience God's grace, God's strength in the midst of difficult times. There was purpose in this trial.

In Mark 8:31-33, Jesus explains to His disciples that God's plan for Him was to suffer and be taken by men and that He must be killed, and then three days later, He would rise. This was confusing to the disciples and so Peter went and rebuked Jesus and said he would not let this happen. Jesus in turn rebukes Peter and confronts him with a very penetrating statement:

"You do not have in mind the concerns of God, but merely human concerns!"

When we consider the motive of prayers, we need to keep in mind the concerns of God, and not be so concerned with our pleasures and desires.

NOTES:

LESSON 15

PRAYING FOR GOD'S PROTECTION

We learn in Psalm 23:1 that *"The Lord is my shepherd."* This means that we are His sheep. Most of us are not very familiar with sheep but they are truly helpless creatures. The shepherd's responsibility is to lead, nurture, and protect the sheep.

In I Peter 2:25 we are told: *"For you were continually straying like sheep, but now you have returned to the Shepherd and Guardian of your souls."* I find it comforting that God's desire is to be my shepherd and the guardian of my soul. However, we have a responsibility in this process.

In Matthew 6:9-13, Jesus is teaching the people to pray, and He gives them the Lord's prayer. It is important to notice how He ends the prayer in verse 13, *"Lead us not into temptation and deliver us from evil."* This is a prayer of spiritual protection, and it seems that if Jesus is instructing us to pray for spiritual protection, we should take it to heart.

I am realizing that this is a practice most Christians have not built into their prayer lives. Evil, the forces of darkness, and Satan do not seem to be much of a threat to modern people. Yet we should clearly take this seriously because we see evil abounding in our culture, and we are foolish to think we cannot fall into temptation.

So, first God wants us to pray for spiritual protection. When Jesus is in the Garden of Gethsemane with Peter, James, and John He says to them:

> Matthew 26:41–*"Keep watching and praying, so that you do not come into temptation; the spirit is willing, but the flesh is weak."*

Then Paul gives us these encouraging words:

> II Thessalonians 3:3–*"But the Lord is faithful, and He will strengthen and protect you from the evil one."*

In order for us to receive this strength and protection from the evil one, we must pray and ask this from God.

As you read the Psalms you also see King David pray for physical protection. In Psalm 27:1, he says *"The Lord is the defense of my life."*

> Psalm 4:8 –*"In peace I will both lie down and sleep, For You alone, Lord, have me dwell in safety."*

> Psalm 18:2,3–*"The Lord is my rock and my fortress and my savior,*

My God, my rock, in whom I take refuge; My shield and the horn of my salvation, my stronghold. I call upon the Lord, who is worthy to be praised, And I am saved from my enemies."

And in the famous Psalm 91, which is a prayer of protection,

Psalm 91:2–4, 11– *"I will say to the Lord, "My refuge and my fortress, My God, in whom I trust! For it is He who rescues you from the net of the trapper and from the deadly plague. He will cover you with His pinions, and under His wings you may take refuge; His faithfulness is a shield and wall. For He will give His angels orders concerning you, to protect you in all your ways."*

I always pray Psalm 121:8 whenever my wife and I are traveling.

Psalm 121:8– *"The Lord will guard your going out and your coming in from this time and forever."*

All of these prayers of protection I pray for myself, my wife, our marriage, our children, and so many of the people who are important in my life.

God desires for us to trust Him with our lives. He instructs us to pray for protection, and when we do, I believe it makes a difference. Who knows, maybe one day the Lord will reveal to us specifically how these prayers made a difference in our lives.

So, I want to encourage you to take these prayers of protection and pray them every day.

NOTES:

HOW TO TALK TO GOD
PART I

I believe a good starting place to pray is to acknowledge who God is and what He has done for us. We are seeking to honor Him, by praising Him. Probably the most famous Psalm of praise in the Bible is Psalm 100. It was historically sung in church worship services. Psalm 100:

> *"Shout joyfully to the LORD, all the earth. Serve the LORD with gladness; Come before Him with rejoicing. Know that the LORD Himself is God; It is He who has made us, and not we ourselves; We are His people and the sheep of His pasture. Enter His gates with thanksgiving, And His courtyards with praise. Give thanks to Him, bless His name. For the LORD is good; His mercy is everlasting, And His faithfulness is to all generations."*

Then Psalm 92 is considered a wonderful praise Psalm for God's goodness. The first verse is very instructive. Psalm 92:1:

> *"It is good to give thanks to the LORD And to sing praises to Your name, Most High;"*

At the heart of praise is giving thanks by God's people. We are called to cultivate a thankful heart and as we do it will change us.

I am talking about spending time each day reflecting upon all that God has done for us and giving Him thanks. As we begin to do this, we will find ourselves giving thanks to Him throughout the day as we see His goodness in our lives.

We see how significant thanksgiving is in Paul's letter to the Colossians church. Colossians 2:6,7:

> *"Therefore, as you have received Christ Jesus the Lord, so walk in Him, having been firmly rooted and now being built up in Him and established in your faith, just as you were instructed, and over-flowing with gratitude."*

This is a picture of the Christian life. You first receive Christ into your life and then you begin to walk with Him through life. Over time your roots will grow into Him, and you will be built up and strengthened in Him. Over time you will become established in your faith. But then notice His instruction, our lives each day should overflow with gratitude.

Then in the next chapter, He give these instructions: Colossians 3:15-17:

"Let the peace of Christ, to which you were indeed called in one body, rule in your hearts; and be thankful. Let the word of Christ richly dwell within you, with all wisdom teaching and admonishing one another with psalms, hymns, and spiritual songs, singing with thankfulness in your hearts to God. Whatever you do in word or deed, do everything in the name of the Lord Jesus, giving thanks through Him to God the Father."

Then Paul says in Colossians 4:2:

"Devote yourselves to prayer, keeping alert in it with an attitude of thanksgiving;"

It is crucial to know that giving thanks to God each day is not only pleasing to Him, but it impacts our lives.

This should not be surprising when you consider the research of Dr. Hans Selye, an Austrian-Canadian endocrinologist who died in 1982. Selye was among the first scientists to discover the impact that emotions play on a person's health. Over his life, he wrote thirty books on the subject of stress and human emotion. At the end of his life, he summarized his research and concluded that a heart of gratitude is the single most nourishing response that leads to good health. Selye believed that thanksgiving and gratitude are therapy for the soul, and that a healthy soul is beneficial to physical health.

As I was doing research on thanksgiving and gratitude, I discovered two recent articles that presented sound arguments on how gratitude has such a powerful impact on our lives. The first article was from Psychology Today and was entitled, "How Gratitude Influences Loving Behavior." The second was from The Wall Street Journal and was entitled, "Thanksgiving and Gratitude: The Science of Happier Holidays." The authors of each of these pieces relied on scientific research to come to their conclusions. What we learn from them is:

• Gratitude is the foundation of satisfying relationships. There is nothing more deadly than when people in a love relationship feel taken for granted.
• Gratitude expresses appreciation. Human interaction flourishes when people feel appreciated.
• People who are the most materialistic in our culture are very ungrateful and extremely unhappy. The relationship between materialism and gratitude run in the opposite direction.
Ungrateful people are clearly unhappy people.

• Gratitude acknowledges all the great benefits of life and enables us to savor all that is good in our lives.

• Finally, and it should come as no surprise, a thankful heart is associated with a number of positive health benefits. Grateful people have stronger immune systems, report fewer symptoms of illness, and enjoy a better quality of sleep. They are also less reactive to stressful events.

For this reason, it is my opinion that thanksgiving should be at the heart of our prayer life, or as Paul put it, "our lives should overflow with gratitude."

NOTES:

HOW TO TALK TO GOD
PART II

S o, what is true thanksgiving? It is simply an expression of gratitude for something received. As Christians it is acknowledging John 3:27:

> *"John replied, "A person can receive not even one thing unless it has been given to him from heaven."*

And James 1:16,17:

> *"Do not be deceived, my beloved brothers and sisters. Every good thing given and every perfect gift is from above, coming down from the Father of lights, with whom there is no variation or shifting shadow."*

Prayerful thanksgiving is acknowledging to God as King David did in I Chronicles 29:4:

> *"all things come from You!"*

So, thanksgiving is acknowledging that every good and perfect gift in life comes from the hand of God. He is the source of all good gifts. This is so crucial that this is ingrained and cultivated into our minds and hearts, because it does not come naturally to us.

What does come natural to us is presumptuousness and ingratitude. This ultimately breeds arrogance and a sense of superiority. Paul confronts this in I Corinthians 4:7:

> *"For who considers you as superior? What do you have that you did not receive? And if you did receive it, why do you boast as if you had not received it?"*

In reality, all that I am and all that I have is a gift of God and I give thanks for it. However, if this is not my perspective on my life and all that I have then what will inevitably happen? Moses reveals the consequences in Deuteronomy 8:17:

> *"Otherwise, you may say in your heart, 'My power and the strength of my hand made me this wealth.'"*

This is so dangerous in the life of a Christian, because if these words become true in your life, then God will become irrelevant, for you believe that everything in your life comes from you and your talent and your strength.

This is why Moses says in the next verse Deuteronomy 8:18:

> *"But you are to remember the Lord your God, for it is He who is giving you power to make wealth, in order to confirm His covenant which He swore to your fathers, as it is this day."*

King David, just before he died, stood before all the assembly, and uttered this prayer to God.

> *"Yours, Lord, is the greatness, the power, the glory, the victory, and the majesty, indeed everything that is in the heavens and on the earth; Yours is the dominion, Lord, and You exalt Yourself as head over all. Both riches and honor come from You, and You rule over all, and in Your hand is power and might; and it lies in Your hand to make great and to strengthen everyone. Now therefore, our God, we thank You, and praise Your glorious name.* —I Chronicles 29:11-13

At the end of his life, David really understood how the hand of God had given him his great wealth and power. This is why some of his last words were: "...we thank You and praise Your glorious name."

NOTES:

HOW TO TALK TO GOD

PART III

I am not sure we realize all that God has blessed us with until we realize the truth that David revealed: *"All things come from You."* (I Chronicles 29:14) A good place to start is to thank God for the gift of your life:

> Revelations 4:11–*"...for You created all things and because of Your will they existed and were created."*

> John 1:3–*"All things came into being through Him, and apart from Him not even one thing came into being that has come into being."*

> Psalm 119:73–*"Your hands made me and fashioned me."*

If you don't thank God for your very existence then in essence you are taking your life for granted, and therefore are taking the Giver of life for granted.

I don't think we realize that not only should we be grateful for the gift of life but also for good health and the fact that God is sustaining our lives.

> Psalm 66:8, 9–*"Bless our God, you peoples, And sound His praise abroad, Who keeps us in life, And does not allow our feet to slip."*

> Psalm 71:6–*"I have leaned on you since my birth; You are He who took me from my mother's womb; My praise is continually of You.*

Here we are declaring to God how much we value our life and health.

We should thank God for our salvation, that He has forgiven us our sin and has given us eternal life.

> I John 2:25–*"This is the promise which He Himself made to us: eternal life."*

> II Corinthians 8:9–*"For you know the grace of our Lord Jesus Christ, that though He was rich, yet for your sake He became poor, so that you through His poverty might become rich."*

> Colossians 1:13,14–*"For He rescued us from the domain of darkness and transferred us to the kingdom of His beloved Son, in whom we have redemption, the forgiveness of sins."*

Not only should we be grateful for our salvation, but for the sacrifice made by Jesus on the cross. How would you thank someone on the field of battle who falls on a hand grenade in a foxhole to save you? This should bring us to our knees as we consider the great price that He paid for the forgiveness of our sins.

We must also consider all the other great spiritual blessings we have been given.

> Ephesians 1:3–*"Blessed be the God and Father of our Lord Jesus Christ, who has blessed us with every spiritual blessing in the heavenly places in Christ,"*

This would include thanking Him for wisdom, His Word, the Holy Spirit, the gift of prayer, His grace, His love, and His guidance. There are so many spiritual gifts that we should offer thanks for.

Think about all the valuable relationships He has blessed us with.

> Proverbs 31:10–*"An excellent wife, who can find her? For her worth is far above jewels."*

> Psalm 127:3–*"Behold, children are a gift of the Lord, The fruit of the womb is a reward."*

> Proverbs 17:17–*"A friend loves at all times."*

I think we all realize life would be bankrupt without our relationships, so we should express our gratitude for them each day.

I think one of the greatest blessings we have in life is our work and the financial resources that are generated. I would again ask you to consider again some of David's last words:

> I Chronicles 29:12,13–*"Both riches and honor come from You, and You rule overall, and in Your hand is power and might; and it lies in Your hand to make great and to strengthen everyone. Now therefore, our God, we thank You, and praise Your glorious name."*

I am struck by Job's famous words in Job 1:21–*"The Lord gives and the Lord takes away, blessed be the name of the Lord."*

We should all consider that whatever God has given us, He can always take away. Therefore, if we will reflect upon all in life that we value, and are not thankful for them and take them for granted, why should we expect God to bless our lives?

PRAYING FOR A CHANGED LIFE

PART I

Have you ever given much thought about the weaknesses in your life? To really understand yourself and the way you live your life, you need to understand these words from the great Christian philosopher Dallas Willard, "We live from the heart." In order to see your life change you must see your heart change.

What do we know about the heart? Solomon tells us this in Proverbs 27:19:

"As water reflects the face, so the heart of man reflects the man."

Jeremiah also tells us the natural state of the human heart: Jeremiah 17:9:

"The heart is more deceitful than all else and is desperately sick; Who can understand it?

So, what are we as humans to do about the sinful state of our hearts? This is where Christianity is so unique, it offers the only solution to the heart.

We see this in the Old Testament where the prophet Ezekiel speaks of what is coming in the future when Jesus arrives and then gives the Holy Spirit to live within us. He says:

Ezekiel 36:26,27–*"I will give you a new heart and put a new spirit in you; I will remove from you your heart of stone and give you a heart of flesh. And I will put my Spirit in you and move you to follow my decrees and be careful to keep my laws."*

What Ezekiel is describing is what Jesus refers to as being born again. He says to Nicodemus in John 3:3: *"...unless one is born again, he cannot see the kingdom of God."* Peter tells us in I Peter 1:3 that God "has caused us to be born again to a living hope."

This is nothing more than your spiritual birth. When a person acknowledges that he is a sinner in need of God's forgiveness and surrenders his heart (repentance), the Holy Spirit then comes into his heart and he experiences the new birth, which is to be born again.

Tim Keller says to be born again is one of life's great blessings from God. We clearly need God's forgiveness, but we also need the Holy Spirit because we are damaged and God desires to repair us and begin a work in our lives.

The new birth that Jesus speaks of is where the Christian life starts, but then what? Paul says in Philippians 1:6:

> *"Being confident of this, that He who began a good work in you will carry it on to completion until the day of Christ Jesus."*

The phrase "began a good work" is a reference to being born again. It is when God began to work in your life and will continue that work until the day you die. It reminds me of a great description of the Christian life, as "God working in the heart of man." There are several important insights about the heart of man for us to consider.

> II Thessalonians 2:16,17–*"Now may our Lord Jesus Christ Himself and God our Father, Who has loved us and given us eternal comfort and good hope by grace, comfort and strengthen your hearts in every good work and word.*
>
> Hebrews 13:9–*"...for it is good for the heart to be strengthened by grace."*

God clearly desires to strengthen our hearts. Yet, He also desires for us to guard our hearts.

> Proverbs 4:23–*"Watch over your heart with all diligence, for from it flow the springs of life."*

God desires us to keep destructive forces from our hearts, for remember, we live from the heart.

God also works in our hearts through the power of the Holy Spirit. Paul tells us in Ephesians 3:16:

> *"I pray that out of His glorious riches He may strengthen you with power through his Spirit in your inner being,"*

The inner being involves your heart.

As we read in an earlier lesson that God uses His Word to penetrate our hearts and it reveals the thoughts and intentions of the heart.

> Hebrews 4:12–*"For the word of God is alive and active. Sharper than any double-edged sword, it penetrates even to dividing soul and spirit, joints, and marrow; it judges the thoughts and attitudes of the heart."*

Finally, I leave you with three verses to consider:

> Proverbs 21:1–*"The king's heart is like channels of water in the hand of the Lord; He turns it wherever He pleases."*

Acts 16:14–*"A woman named Lydia was listening; she was a seller of purple fabrics from the city of Thyatira, and a worshiper of God. [a] The Lord opened her heart to respond to the things spoken by Paul."*

Nehemiah 7:5–*"So, God put it in my heart to assemble the nobles."*

These verses indicate that God and only God can move in our hearts, transform the heart, open the heart, turn the heart, and incline the heart. In the next lesson, we will look at how God uses prayer to accomplish this.

NOTES:

PRAYING FOR A CHANGED LIFE
PART II

I n this lesson we want to consider the transformation of our lives through prayer. I would like you to consider this scripture and pay close attention to the wording.

Look at David's prayer about the inclination of his heart in Psalm 141:4:

"Do not incline my heart to any evil thing to practice deeds of wickedness."

Then observe his prayer in Psalm 51:10:

"Do not incline my heart to any evil thing, to practice deeds of wickedness with people who do wrong; And may I not taste their delicacies."

There is a wonderful prayer in Psalm 119:36 -

"Incline my heart to Your testimonies, And not to dishonest gain."

Then in Psalm 138:3 -

"When I called, You answered me, you made me bold and stouthearted."

In Jeremiah 24:7 God says:

"I will give them a heart to want to know Me."

This can be converted to a prayer request.

Observe Solomon's prayer to God in I Kings 8:58:

"That the Lord may incline our hearts to Himself to walk in all His ways and keep His commandments."

Finally, consider Paul's words which are like a prayer in I Thessalonians 3:12,13:

"and may the Lord cause you to increase and overflow in love for one another, and for all people, just as we also do for you; so that He may establish your hearts blameless in holiness before our God and Father at the coming of our Lord Jesus with all His saints."

As we consider the transformation of the heart, it is worth examining these words from C. S. Lewis:

"As we grow spiritually and become more like Christ, we better understand and see the true, deprived condition of the heart, and how far we have to go (this can create frustration in us). However, when there is no real spiritual growth in our lives, as we spiritually drift, we become less and less aware of our sinfulness. The more we seek to deal with our sinfulness, the better we will understand ourselves. Obedience to God brings light into our lives, indulgence to sin brings a fog."

Finally, in order to see our weaknesses and our sins so that we can pray for God to work in our hearts, we need to be aware of them.

Look at David's prayer in Psalm 139:23, 24:

> *"Search me, God, and know my heart; Put me to the test and know my anxious thoughts; And see if there is any hurtful way in me and lead me in the everlasting way."*

Then you see Jesus's powerful words in Matthew 7:3-5:

> *"Why do you look at the speck that is in your brother's eye, but do not notice the log that is in your own eye? Or how can you say to your brother, 'Let me take the speck out of your eye,' and look, the log is in your own eye? You hypocrite, first take the log out of your own eye, and then you will see clearly to take the speck out of your brother's eye!"*

I often pray that God will show me the logs in my life and ask Him to show me what is true of my heart. I ask Him to show me my sin. This I believe is crucial if we are to know what to pray for regarding the condition of our heart.

NOTES:

PRAYING FOR A CHANGED LIFE
PART III

As we consider our flaws and weaknesses, we need to remember we are incapable of changing our hearts. This is why we must recognize where we struggle and then look to God to transform our hearts through our prayer life.

I am going to consider a number of issues that we need to be praying about. This is not an all-inclusive list but will serve as a guide to help you along the way. This is a good place to start.

> • In Philippians 2:3, 4–*"Do nothing from selfishness or empty conceit, but with humility consider one another as more important than yourselves; do not merely look out for your own personal interests, but also for the interests of others."*

A prayer to consider is "Lord I pray that You would deliver me from self-centeredness, and that I would put others in front of myself.

> • Hebrews 13:5–*"Make sure that your character is free from the love of money, being content with what you have; for He Himself has said, "I will never desert you, nor will I ever abandon you,"*
>
> Psalm 62:10–*"Do not trust in oppression, And do not vainly rely on robbery; If wealth increases, do not set your heart on it."*

"Lord, I pray that You would deliver my heart from the love of money and that I would be content with what I have."

> • Galatians 1:10–*"For am I now seeking the favor of people, or of God? Or am I striving to please people? If I were still trying to please people, I would not be a bondservant of Christ."*

"Lord, I pray that You would deliver me from the desire to impress others, to win man's approval. Help me to keep all my achievements and accomplishments a secret."

> • James 4:12–*"There is only one Lawgiver and Judge, the One who is able to save and to destroy; but who are you, judging your neighbor?"*
>
> Matthew 7:1–*"Do not judge, so that you will not be judged."*

"Lord, I pray that you would deliver me from self-righteousness and judging others. We all are fighting different battles, help me to have compassion on those who are different from me."

• Anger is a serious problem in the lives of many people. We generally get angry when things don't go our way. What we fail to realize is that anger can leave a mark on our souls. These verses can be used in our prayer life.

James 1:19–*"You know this, my beloved brothers and sisters. Now everyone must be quick to hear, slow to speak, and slow to anger.*

"Lord, help me to be quick to listen, slow to speak, and slow to anger."

Proverbs 16:32–*"One who is slow to anger is better than the mighty, And one who rules his spirit, than one who captures a city."*

Ecclesiastes 7:9–*"Do not be eager in your spirit to be angry, for anger resides in the heart of fools."*

• We need to ask God to help us be committed to the truth and to hate falsehood.

Psalm 24:3,4–*"Who may ascend onto the hill of the Lord? And who may stand in His holy place? One who has clean hands and pure heart, who has not lifted up his soul to deceit and has not sworn deceitfully."*

• We should also ask God to help us with the quality of our words.

Ephesians 4:29–*"Do not let any unwholesome talk come out of your mouths, but only what is helpful for building others up according to their needs, that it may benefit those who listen.*

• For men, who particularly struggle with sexual lust and temptation, we should pray for specific protection. This would include a struggle with pornography.

I Thessalonians 4:3,4–*"For this is the will of God, your sanctification; that is, that you abstain from sexual immorality; that each of you know how to possess his own vessel in sanctification and honor."*

Psalm 101:4–*"A perverse heart shall leave me; I will know no evil."*

II Thessalonians 3:3 – *"But the Lord is faithful, and He will strengthen and protect you from the evil one."*

• Pray for your marriage. First, ask God to give you the wisdom to better love your spouse.

Proverbs 5:18,19–*"Let your fountain be blessed, and rejoice in the wife of your youth. As a loving hind and a graceful doe, let her breasts satisfy you at all times; Be exhilarated always with her love."*

Ask that God would give you eyes only for your spouse.

Psalm 67:1–*"God be gracious to us and bless us and cause His face to shine upon us."*

Pray for God's blessing and favor to be upon your marriage.

• Pray for your children.

Proverbs 2:10–*"For wisdom will enter your heart, and knowledge will be delightful to your soul;"*

Pray Isaiah 44:3 for your children.

"For I will pour water on the thirsty land and streams on the dry ground; I will pour out My Spirit on your offspring, and My blessing on your descendants."

• Business Life

Psalm 67:1–*"God be gracious to us and bless us, and cause His face to shine upon us."*

Psalm 31:3–*"For You are my rock and my fortress; For the sake of Your name, You will lead me and guide me."*

James 1:5–*"But if any of you lacks wisdom, let him ask of God, Who gives to all generously and without reproach, and it will be given to him."*

If God desires to give us wisdom, insight, and direction shouldn't we be seeking it? This too must come through our prayer life.

• There are many other issues to pray over.

Psalm 39:4 – *"Lord, let me know my end, And what is the extent of my days; Let me know how transient I am."*

Psalm 90:12–*"So teach us to number our days, that we may present to You a heart of wisdom."*

"Lord, help me to keep in mind how short this life is so that I might not waste my time."

Pray for others in your life who have great needs. The Apostle Paul prayed for many of the Christians who had established early churches. C. S. Lewis spent a large amount of time praying for others.

Over the years, I have seen many Christians who think they don't have much to pray about. From all these lessons on prayer, I hope you see there is much that we can be praying for.

NOTES:

THE TRIUNE GOD

The God of the Bible is one God in three distinct persons: God the Father, God the Son, and God the Holy Spirit. The best way to comprehend this is to consider water, H2O. In other words, H2O can be liquid water that you drink, it can be frozen and therefore solid ice, or it can be a gas when it is heated and becomes steam. So, H2O can be liquid, solid, or steam but they are all H2O.

In the Bible you see the predominance of God the Father in the Old Testament. In the New Testament, the first four books are called the Gospels (Matthew, Mark, Luke, and John) and in these books you see the predominance of God the Son, Jesus. Once Christ leaves the earth you see the coming of the Holy Spirit at Pentecost (Acts 2) and from that point forward, you see the Holy Spirit at work in the lives of Christians.

As you read the four Gospel books on Jesus' life, you notice that Christ speaks often of His relationship with God the Father. Rarely does He mention the Holy Spirit. Then, right before He is taken and crucified, Christ unleashes a great deal of teaching on the Holy Spirit and the work He will do in their lives and in the lives of all believers.

In John 14, Jesus tells the 12 disciples that He is soon going to leave them but that He will be replaced by the Holy Spirit who He calls "The Counselor." Other translations call Him "the Helper."

> John 14:16,17–*"I will ask the Father, and He will give you another Helper, so that He may be with you forever; the Helper is the Spirit of truth, whom the world cannot receive, because it does not see Him or know Him; but you know Him because He remains with you and will be in you."*

The Helper/Counselor comes from the Greek word, "paracletos" which means "one who comes along to help you." The Holy Spirit wants to be our helper.

Jesus then mentions the coming of the Holy Spirit again in John 15:26:

> *"When the Helper comes, whom I will send to you from the Father, namely, the Spirit of truth who comes from the Father, He will testify about Me."*

And then in John 16:7, 8, He mentions the Helper again.

"But I tell you the truth: it is to your advantage that I am leaving; for if I do not leave, the Helper will not come to you; but if I go, I will send Him to you. And He, when He comes, will convict the world regarding sin, and righteousness, and judgment:"

Think about this, Jesus had been with them for three years, rarely ever mentioning the Holy Spirit. Then He pours out all this teaching, which they did not really understand. Jesus was trying to comfort them by the fact that I am going to be with you, not in human form as I have been, but in Spirit.

I think it is important to look at Jesus' final words to the disciples before He leaves them:

Luke 24:44-49–44–*Now He said to them, "These are My words which I spoke to you while I was still with you, that all the things that are written about Me in the Law of Moses and the Prophets and the Psalms must be fulfilled." Then He opened their minds to understand the Scriptures, and He said to them, "So it is written, that the Christ would suffer and rise from the dead on the third day, and that repentance for forgiveness of sins would be proclaimed in His name to all the nations, beginning from Jerusalem. You are witnesses of these things. And behold, I am sending the promise of My Father upon you; but you are to stay in the city until you are clothed with power from on high."*

In verse 44, He explains that this is what He has been trying to teach them these past three years. He goes through all the Messianic prophecies in the Old Testament. Most significantly, He wanted them to know that He did not come to be an earthly king. He came not only as the Messiah, but a suffering Messiah, a sin bearing Messiah that rose from the dead. It was all foretold in the Old Testament.

In verse 47, He tells them the message that they were to take out into the world is *"repentance for the forgiveness of sin."*

And then, in verse 49, He tells them the Holy Spirit would soon be unleashed into their lives. But as we learn in the rest of the New Testament, this same spirit can be unleashed in the lives of all believers.

NOTES:

THE POWER OF THE HOLY SPIRIT
PART I

The last words of Jesus to His disciples in Luke 24:49 is that they were "to stay in the city (Jerusalem) until you are clothed with the power from on high." Jesus was referring to the coming of the Holy Spirit.

In Acts 2, we see the unleashing of the Holy Spirit on a special Jewish holy day called Pentecost. It was like a violent rushing wind. Peter then proceeds to deliver a powerful sermon in Acts 2:14-41. In verse 38, he tells the crowd of people listening to this sermon *"...and you shall receive the gift of the Holy Spirit."*

I know I mentioned this in an earlier lesson but once a person acknowledges they are sinners and then repents, the Holy Spirit literally comes into that person's life.

Galatians 4:6–*"...God has sent forth the Spirit of His Son into our hearts..."*

Romans 5:5–*"...the love of God has been poured out within our hearts through the Holy Spirit who was given us."*

So, God the Holy Spirit resides in us and is the mark of a true Christian. In Romans 8:9, Paul tells us that "if we do not have the Spirit of Christ in us, we do not belong to Him." In Ephesians 1:13, Paul refers to it as being "sealed" with the Holy Spirit.

It is important that we see why this is one of the greatest spiritual blessings of life. Listen to what Paul says:

Philippians 4:13–*"I can do all things through Him who strengthens me."*

Ephesians 6:10–*"Finally, be strong in the Lord and in the strength of His might."*

In both verses Paul speaks of the spiritual strength that God desires to give us. But how does He do this? Through the power of the Holy Spirit.

Ephesians 3:16–*"that He would grant you, according to the riches of His glory, to be strengthened with power through His Spirit i the inner self."*

Ephesians 3:20–*"Now to Him who is able to do far more abundantly beyond all that we ask or think, according to the power that works within us."*

Then Paul tells us how we find joy and peace, which all modern people are searching for, through the power of the Holy Spirit.

Romans 15:13–*"Now may the God of hope fill you with all joy and peace in believing, so that you will abound in hope by the power of the Holy Spirit."*

It is important to know that there is a difference between the Spirit coming into your life at salvation and the Spirit flowing through you, filling you, and empowering you. We get this idea of the Spirit flowing through us in an illustration that Jesus gives us:

John 15:1-5–*"I am the true vine, and My Father is the vinedresser. Every branch in Me that does not bear fruit, He takes away; and every branch that bears fruit, He prunes it so that it may bear more fruit. You are already clean because of the word which I have spoken to you. Abide in Me, and I in you. Just as the branch cannot bear fruit of itself but must abide in the vine, so neither can you unless you abide in Me. I am the vine, you are the branches; the one who abides in Me, and I in him bears much fruit, for apart from Me you can do nothing."*

This is a picture of the relationship between a vine and its branches. The main focus is not mentioned but clearly implied. Jesus is speaking of the sap that flows from the vine into the branch. This is a picture of God's Spirit flowing into our lives, just as sap flows from a vine into the branch.

NOTES:

THE POWER OF THE HOLY SPIRIT

PART II

A s you read through the book of Acts and Paul's letters you see phrases such as being filled with the Spirit or walking in the power of the Holy Spirit.

Some examples are:

> Acts 4:8– *'...Peter was filled with the Holy Spirit."*

> Acts 4:31– *"...they were all filled with the Holy Spirit."*

> Acts 13:9– *"...Paul was filled with the Holy Spirit..."*

> Acts 13:52– *"And the disciples were continually filled with joy and with the Holy Spirit."*

Notice it was a daily continuous process.

> Galatians 5:16– *"But I say, walk by the Spirit, and you will not carry out the desire of the flesh."*

If you keep reading, Paul contrasts operating in the power of the flesh versus walking or being filled with the power of the Spirit. He ends in verses 22 and 23 listing the fruit of the Spirit, love, joy, and peace.

> Galatians 5:25– *"If we live by the Spirit, let us walk by the Spirit."*

> Ephesians 5:18– *"Do not get drunk on wine, which leads to debauchery. Instead, be filled with the Spirit."*

The literal translation of the last phrase is "Keep on being filled."

Dr. Lewis Sperry Chafer, a great theologian, and the first president of Dallas Theological Seminary, also reflects on this passage from Ephesians:

"Being filled with the Spirit is compared to intoxication in which wine affects the entire person, both the mental activity of the mind and the physical activity of the body. The filling of the Spirit (like intoxication) is not a once for all experience. The Christian therefore is daily dependent upon God for empowering by the continuous filling of the Spirit."

Chafer continues with:

"To be filled with the Spirit is related to Christian experience, power, and service (bearing fruit.) [The Spirit comes into the life of the believer at salvation, once and for all.] But the filling of the Spirit is a repeated experience and is mentioned frequently in the Bible.

Beginning with the day of Pentecost, a new age dawned in which the Holy Spirit would work in every believer. Now those Christians who had the Spirit of God in them could be filled by the Spirit if he met the conditions. Numerous illustrations in the New Testament confirm this."

He goes on to say:

"There is an observable difference in the character and quality of the daily life of Christians. Few can be categorized as being full of the Spirit. This lack, however, is not due to failure on the part of God to make provision, but rather failure on the part of the individual to appropriate and permit the Spirit of God to fill his life."

NOTES:

THE POWER OF THE HOLY SPIRIT
PART III

In Lesson 24, we looked at some very significant words in John 15, where Jesus provides an illustration of a vine and a branch. The key visual to the illustration is the sap flowing from the vine, into the branch. This is a picture of the Holy Spirit flowing from the vine into us, the branch.

There is another very important metaphor that Jesus employs from John 7:37-39, where He gives us an explanation of the Spirit flowing into us by making reference to rivers of living water. This is what Jesus actually says:

> *"Now on the last day, the great day of the feast, Jesus stood and cried out, saying, 'If any man is thirsty, let him come to Me and drink. He who believes in Me, as the Scripture said, 'From his innermost being shall flow rivers of living water.' But this He spoke of the Spirit, whom those who believed in Him were to receive; for the Spirit was not yet given, because Jesus was not yet glorified."*

The Amplified version of the Bible says, "the rivers of living water will flow continuously."

The person who shared the significance of these three verses with me is my good friend and mentor John Riddle.

"Before we talk about the passage, we need to understand the context in which it occurred. The people were celebrating the Feast of the Tabernacles which was held annually to remember God's supernatural provision for Israel during the forty years in the wilderness when manna and water were provided, clothes did not wear out, etc. The purpose of the feast was to express appreciation to God for survival of the nation during those years. On the last day of the feast, all males within 90 miles of Jerusalem were required to appear at the temple. The high priest poured out water from a pitcher, reminding the people of the promise in Joel 2:28, 29 where God promised to pour out His Spirit so that the people would serve Him in power."

The scripture in Joel that he refers to is quoted by Peter at Pentecost. In Acts 2:17, Peter says, *"And it shall be in the last days that I will pour forth my spirit on all mankind."* Joel spoke these words in the ninth century B.C., predicting that at some point in the future, God would make the outpouring of His Spirit available to all mankind.

Going back to John 7:37, Jesus says: *"if anyone is thirsty,"* What is thirst?

It is an indication of a need. We have to start by approaching God with a sense of neediness. We need to approach Him with this prayer:

"Lord, I need Your power in my life."

In one sense, this is an emptying of ourselves so that we may be filled with the Spirit.

So, it starts with *"If any man is thirsty."* Jesus then says, *"let him come to Me."* We are to go to Him, the source of power, the source of peace that we are seeking. But how does a person approach God? It starts with humility.

In James 4:8, we are told:

"Draw near to God and He will draw near to you. Cleanse your hands you sinners and purify your hearts you double-minded."

In the book, *The Power of a Humble Life*, I wrote about this scripture in James 4:

"The book of James gives some insight into the relationship between humility, humbling ourselves, and confession of sin. In James 4:6, we are told God is opposed to the proud but gives grace to the humble. In verse eight, we are told to draw near to God and He will draw near to us. He says that before we can draw near, as sinners we must cleanse our hands and our hearts. We need to cleanse ourselves from not only the outer sins that people see but also the inner sins of the heart. As one commentator put it, 'Your hands and heart symbolize your deeds and thoughts.' Therefore, in order to really draw near to God, we must cleanse ourselves, and this is done by the confession of sin. Confessing our sin is, as Jesus said, a way we humble ourselves before God."

Finally in verse 37, Jesus tells us to drink. This simply is to ask God to fill us with the Holy Spirit.

Jesus says in Luke 11:13:

"If you then being evil know how to give good gifts to your children, how much more will your heavenly Father give the Holy Spirit to those who ask."

Notice this is not asking Christ into your life for salvation. The reason we know this is because you are asking your heavenly Father. This is a Christian asking God his Father to fill him.

When we ask God to fill us with His Spirit, it's as if God turns on a valve so that His power flows into our lives. It is like the sap of the vine flowing into the branch.

There is only one thing that cuts off the flow of the Spirit, and that is when we sin. John Riddle puts it this way:

"The power of the Holy Spirit will continue to flow through us until we sin again. Our sin shuts the valves off, and the flow stops. The Holy Spirit is still residing in us, but His power is not flowing through us. We are back to operating in the power of the flesh. When we are aware of this, we must go through the steps of reentering this abiding relationship."

I find myself having to re-enter this abiding relationship throughout the day because of my sinfulness. Yet, I can say this has been a life-changing teaching, dramatically impacting my life over the last 35 years.

NOTES:

LESSON 26

BUILDING A STRONG FOUNDATION

I read a humorous story by Dr. Tony Evans.

"I went to the Leaning Tower of Pisa when I was in Italy. If you're ever in Italy, don't bother going to Pisa. That had to be the biggest disappointment of my trip. You see these newscasts with the Leaning Tower of Pisa imposingly behind the newscaster. You get to Pisa, and it ain't that big. I spent my time and money, my energy, and my effort to watch a building lean. Another reason you ought not to go to Pisa is there ain't nothing in Pisa but that tower. So don't be looking for other stuff to do. There is nothing to do in Pisa but watch a tower lean and watch vendors selling you replicas of towers that lean. Do you know why the tower in Pisa leans? The Leaning Tower of Pisa leans because it's located in Pisa. Pisa means marshy. The tower was built in a marsh, on mud. It did not have the proper foundation. And because it did not have the proper foundation, it was not able to remain stable, and every year it would lean another 1/20th of an inch. When we were there, they had ropes all around it, holding it until they could do something about this ongoing leaning. If it continued, in seven years it would collapse. It was built on the wrong foundation. The only thing the Leaning Tower of Pisa is good for are tourists. All it is is for show, for people to come by and look at it."

In the *Sermon on the Mount* Jesus tells us we are all building our lives on some type of foundation.

> Matthew 7:24-27–*"Therefore, everyone who hears these words of Mine, and acts on them, will be like a wise man who built his house on the rock. And the rain fell, and the floods came, and the winds blew and slammed against that house; and yet it did not fall, for it had been founded on the rock. And everyone who hears these words of Mine, and does not act on them, will be like a foolish man who built his house on the sand. And the rain fell, and the floods came, and the winds blew and slammed against that house; and it fell—and its collapse was great."*

In these verses Jesus is telling each one of us that storms are coming into our lives sometime in the future, we just don't know when.

Solomon reminds us in Proverbs 27:1:

> *"Do not boast about tomorrow, For you do not know what a day*

may bring."

So, no one is exempt. The good news is that we can be prepared when they do come.

It is important to know that everyone is building a house with their life. We are constructing a strategy that we believe will best prepare us for the future. Both men in this illustration are erecting a life, a life they both think is worth living, that is significant and is going somewhere.

Philip Yancey says the best way to prepare for the storms of life is to work on a strong, supportive life when all is going well. You cannot suddenly construct a foundation of inner strength. It must be built day by day.

This is such a significant issue because the storms of life, or potential storms, are what generate fear in our lives. We fear the uncertainty of the outcome of these storms.

Throughout the Bible we see God telling and instructing us to "Fear not; do not be afraid; Be anxious about nothing; Let your heart not be troubled."

> Isaiah 41:20– *"Do not fear, for I am with you; Do not be afraid, for I am your God. I will strengthen you, I will also help you, I will also uphold you with My righteous right hand."*

We are told not to fear. This is not what God wants for our lives. He hates what fear does to us.

Think about the harm it does to human life. It brings stress that can harm your health and keep you from sleeping.

Solomon tells us in Proverbs 14:30:

> *"A heart of peace gives life to the body."*

Fear has a huge impact on us psychologically. It runs wild in our imagination and strangles the mind's ability to think clearly. Fear can often bring depression into our lives.

Finally, fear and worry impact us spiritually. Jesus tells us in the Parable of the Sower and the seeds that worry is one of the things that chokes the Word of God and leaves us unfruitful.

In Luke 21:34, Jesus instructs us to be on our guard that our hearts would not be weighed down by the *"worries of life."*

Clearly, fear and worry can do great harm to our lives, and this is why we are instructed to *"fear not."*

NOTES:

THE STORMS OF LIFE
PART I

One of the most significant statements I have ever read on why humans struggle with life comes from the famous French mathematician and philosopher Blaise Pascal. He says one of the primary reasons people struggle with life is because they have false ideas about reality.

I share this because I believe it is so easy for Christians to have a false understanding and a false perspective on the storms of life and how God uses them purposefully in the lives of His children.

I would like for you to consider some scripture that is pertinent to this issue:

> Isaiah 55:8,9–*"For My thoughts are not your thoughts, Nor are your ways My ways," declares the Lord. "For as the heavens are higher than the earth, So are My ways higher than your ways."*

> Psalm 50:21–*"When you did these things and I kept silent, you thought I was exactly like you..."*

God is not like us; He does not think the way we think. He does not see life the way we do. He does not see painful and troubling circumstances as we do. God's ways and plans are so much higher and grander than ours.

One of the reasons is because of God's perspective on time, which is so different from ours. Most of us are planning and focusing on the next five, ten, or twenty years of life. Think of God's perspective on time.

> II Peter 3:8–*"But do not let this one fact escape your notice, beloved, that with the Lord one day is like a thousand years, and a thousand years like one day."*

We need to realize that ultimately God's time horizon is eternal, He cares about our eternal well-being. He sees what we don't see, and His thoughts and plans are so much higher than ours.

This next truth is so important to grasp as we consider the storms of life. This story will help us understand it.

Dr. Henry K. Beecher of Harvard Medical School made an interesting observation among the 215 wounded men from the Anzio beachhead in World War II:

Only one in four soldiers with serious injuries (fractures, amputations, penetrated chests, or cerebrums) asked for morphine, though it was freely available. They simply did not need help with the pain, and indeed many of them denied feeling pain at all. Beecher, an anesthesiologist, contrasted the soldiers' reactions to what he had seen in private practice, where 80 percent of patients recovering from surgical wounds begged for morphine or other narcotics.

Here you have two different groups of people suffering from the same exact injuries. The soldiers' responses to pain were impacted by the fact that their injuries carried with them a sense of meaning – a result of being involved in a significant mission for their country. They also had a sense of gratitude that they had survived. Yet the civilian patients with the same exact wounds saw their injuries as being depressing and calamitous, and thus "they begged for morphine or other narcotics."

Just hours before Jesus was taken into custody, He made this point to His disciples in John 16:21:

> *"Whenever a woman is in labor, she has pain, because her hour has come; but when she gives birth to the child, she no longer remembers the anguish because of the joy that a child has been born into the world."*

A mother's pain produces something with meaning, a new life, and for that reason she can even contemplate repeating the experience without fear and worry. The point I am making is so crucial to grasp. It is foundational if you are going to effectively deal with fear.

In the midst of the storms of life we will either allow what we are experiencing to influence our view of God, or we will allow our view of God to influence what we are experiencing. We must understand that God has made it eminently clear that there is purpose in our pain and suffering. With this perspective we can find purpose behind the circumstances causing our fear.

This explains the very counter-intuitive words of James 1:2-4:

> *"Consider it pure joy, my brothers and sisters, whenever you face trials of many kinds, because you know that the testing of your faith produces perseverance. Let perseverance finish its work so that you may be mature and complete, not lacking anything."*

NOTES:

THE STORMS OF LIFE
PART II

A big question that we all should consider is what do I need to know about God that will enable me to properly interpret what I am experiencing in the storms of life? What do I need to know about God that will transform my fear into peace?

First, we should remember that God is our heavenly Father. Jesus makes it clear in Matthew 7:11 that His love for us is far greater than the love we have for our own children. That is hard to fathom.

Jesus tells us in Matthew 6:25:

> *"not to be worried about our lives and circumstances."* Then in verse 26:

> *"Look at the birds of the air; they do not sow or reap or store away in barns, and yet your heavenly Father feeds them. Are you not much more valuable than they?"*

He tells us how He cares for the birds in the air but considers how much more valuable we are to Him.

In Jeremiah 31:3, God tells us:

> *"I have loved you with an everlasting love."*

We also learn from King David that God our Father is committed to us and our well-being and that we are of incredible value to Him.

In Psalm 56:8-11 He says:

> *"You have taken account of my miseries; Put my tears in Your bottle. Are they not in Your book? Then my enemies will turn back on the day when I call; This I know that God is for me. In God, whose word I praise, In the Lord, whose word I praise, In God I have put my trust, I shall not be afraid. What can mankind do to me?"*

A crucial verse that enables us to see a vital truth in this teaching is in Matthew 10:29 where Jesus says:

> *"Are not two sparrows sold for a penny? Yet not one of them will fall to the ground outside your Father's care."*

What we glean from this verse is that if there is a storm in our lives it is there with God's consent. Furthermore, it is not surprising that God tells us in Jeremiah 32:27:

> *""Behold, I am the Lord, the God of all flesh; is anything too difficult for Me?"*

Clearly, God could remove any difficulty from our lives whenever He chooses. Therefore, we should conclude that the storms of life are present in our lives because they have a purpose.

A verse that has meant a great deal to me and helped me understand how God purposefully uses storms is in Paul's words in Romans 8:28:

> *"And we know that God causes all things to work together for good to those who love God, to those who are called according to His purpose."*

These words gave me a great deal of encouragement to see that whatever storm might enter my life as a Christian, God is going to cause it to work together for my good.

The problem with me was how to interpret the word "good". Sure, I wanted the "good life" and thought that was what God wanted for me. However, I had interpreted the good life to mean achievement, comfort, pleasure, and prosperity.

After it was pointed out to me, I soon realized the importance of looking at the next verse in Romans because verse 29 revealed what was actually good for my life in the sight of God. What I considered to be the good life was not at all what God had revealed it to be. In Romans 8:29 we are told what the ultimate good in life is to:

> *"Become conformed to the image of His Son..."*

The ultimate good in life is to become like Christ. Now, I realize we live in a culture where men might not believe Christlikeness is very manly. I know for many years it did not have much appeal for me. In my mind, it meant I had to be more religious, that I had to withdraw from the world and go into hiding. This is not what I desired for my life.

However, as I studied Jesus' life, I began to realize Jesus was not religious—at least not what we typically think of as being religious. He lived in a very religious culture, where many of the religious people found Him to be quite contemptible:

- He did not follow their traditions to the letter of the Law.
- Many of the religious leaders did not like the people He hung out with,
- He spoke harshly to the Pharisees and other men of learning and status.

• He made political matters worse as many of their followers began to follow Him and His teachings.

God is asking us to strive to be like Christ in all our thoughts, words, and deeds. Christlikeness is the objective, and I would readily share that such a life is not a life of self-righteousness or the absence of achievement and pleasure. Over the years, what I have come to recognize is that what Christ is simply instructing each of us to do is:

• To be transformed in our character
• To grow in wisdom
• To love, to have compassion, and to have quality relationships.

Character, wisdom, and love make up the essence of what it means to be Christlike, what it ultimately means to be an authentic man.

NOTES:

THE STORMS OF LIFE
PART III

I f we have been told that God is causing all things, particularly the storms of life, to work together for our good, then all the storms that came into my life have purpose. If that is the case, then I should be thankful.

This is why James says to consider it all joy to experience various trials because of its powerful influence on our spiritual lives. James knew trials would be used by God to develop us spiritually and that we should respond joyfully.

So, how does thanksgiving play a role in our response to trials and difficulty? The Apostle Paul says in Philippians 4:6,7:

> *"Do not be anxious about anything, but in every situation, by prayer and petition, with thanksgiving, present your requests to God. And the peace of God, which transcends all understanding, will guard your hearts and your minds in Christ Jesus."*

And then in I Thessalonians 5:18:

> *"Give thanks in all circumstances; for this is God's will for you in Christ Jesus."*

When you are in the midst of a storm and you have no idea how it's going to turn out nor how God is going to use it for good in your life, thanksgiving places confidence in God and the ultimate outcome. It is an act of faith, as you trust Him with the outcome and are confident that He is going to use it for good in your life. Paul tells us in Philippians that this is essential in experiencing God's peace.

Consider approaching Him with this perspective and prayer:

"Lord, I don't know what You are doing in my life or why You have allowed this, but I thank You for how You are going to use this purposefully in my life."

"I pray that what I am experiencing will lead to spiritual growth, inner transformation, and a deeper relationship with You. And I thank You that You will bring this to pass."

This is what it means to walk by faith, trusting Him with your circumstances and the ultimate outcome. When you do this, God begins to move in your life by giving you strength and peace. He also might choose to move in the circumstances that are causing fear and pain.

Please know God loves it when we, His children, trust Him and walk by faith. We are told in Hebrews 11:6:

"Without faith, it is impossible for us to please Him."

I love the story in the life of the Russian Nobel Prize winning author Aleksandr Solzhenitsyn. In his 20's he was thrown into prison after making some critical remarks about Joseph Stalin. He entered prison as an atheist, but at some point, had a powerful conversion experience and became a Christian. He concluded that God used severe hardship to make a spiritual breakthrough in his life. He saw how purposeful going to prison was in his life. As he walked out of prison after serving an eight-year sentence, he uttered these powerful words:

"I bless you, prison. I bless you for being in my life. For there, lying on the rotting prison straw, I learned the object of life is not prosperity as I had grown up believing, but the maturing of the soul."

How could anyone consider eight years in prison a blessing? Eight years separated from one's family and friends. Solzhenitsyn realized God had made a spiritual breakthrough in his life through prison. A breakthrough otherwise might never have happened. Instead of being angry and bitter, Solzhenitsyn was grateful.

NOTES:

THE STORMS OF LIFE
PART IV

There are two final truths for us to consider about the storms of life. The first has to do with the actual storm. Counselor and author Julie Sparkman says that we all have a "picture" of how we want life to be. Your "picture" involves people in your life and your circumstances. When your "picture" (the way you want life to be) and your circumstances are aligned, life is good, because everything is going the way you want it to go. However, when or if your "picture" blows up, it brings pressure, stress, pain, and fear into your life.

Jesus gives us sound instructions for this in Matthew 11:28-30:

> *"Come to Me, all who are weary and heavy-laden, and I will give you rest. Take My yoke upon you and learn from Me, for I am gentle and humble in heart, and you will find rest for you souls. For My yoke is easy and My burden is light."*

Jesus is telling us to surrender our yoke to Him, and then take His yoke. Applying this teaching to our picture, Jesus is saying surrender your picture to Me and take My picture. Accept the picture I have for you.

One could ask, "Why?" Because God is in control. As we look at our shattered pictures, He tell us that He is not absent. He is in our circumstances, saying, "I am with you." Furthermore, as a Christian, He is in me. His Holy Spirit resides in me.

Going back to Jesus' words in Matthew 11, we must understand the purpose of a yoke back in Biblical times. It provided the means of harnessing the effort of two animals to accomplish a common objective. It is crucial during times when your picture and reality are not in alignment that we embrace God's yoke. Although it's a natural reaction for us to beg Him to give us our picture, we should embrace God's yoke, God's objective in our circumstance.

Our prayer should be, "Lord, I am committed to You and Your objective for my life. I am with You in whatever You are trying to accomplish in me."

We should also ask Him, what is my role in this; what would You have me do?

The second and final truth I leave you on the storms of life which creates all types of fear, is some simple instruction from Jesus in Matthew 6:34:

> *"So do not worry about tomorrow, for tomorrow will care for itself.*

Each day has enough of its own."

Jesus is contrasting tomorrow versus today. The future and the present. Worry and fear are clearly about tomorrow and the uncertainty over what is going to happen tomorrow.

Author and scholar David Wells wrote the following passage on fear and modern life. He says:

"The world intrudes upon us as it never has before. One of the surest indications of this is that the levels of anxiety have never been higher. And why are we more anxious? There are, no doubt, many reasons, including a heightened tempo in the workplace, greater economic insecurity, too many choices, and perhaps family breakdown. What is more, the extraordinary rapidity of change in our society powerfully fixes our attention on the future, for we need to anticipate events that are in the making in order to avoid what will be harmful and to capitalize on what will be beneficial. Anxiety, however, is nothing more than living out the future before it arrives, and modernity obliges us to do this many times over. The future is thereby greatly intensified for us."

Jesus provides us with wise guidance as He stresses the importance of living in the present, focused on the day in front of us. As we are encouraged by the Psalmist, *"This is the day that the Lord has made, let us rejoice and be glad in this day."* (Psalm 118:24) Not tomorrow.

When we are weighed down over the uncertainty over what is going to happen tomorrow, humbly go before Christ and ask Him:

"Lord, I pray that you will give me the grace to live one day at a time. That I might live in the present as You have instructed me. I realize I can't do this on my own, so I look to You to enable me to do that which I cannot do myself."

NOTES:

GOD'S LIGHT

There is a wonderful verse in Psalm 119:105 that says, *"Your word is a lamp to my feet and a light to my path."* And then, we are told in Psalm 18:28, *"For You light my lamp, the Lord my God illumines my darkness."*

One of the major themes in the Bible is the contrast of light and darkness. The reason is because a Christian sees life differently. We see life through the lens of God's truth. God desires that we become wise, because wisdom is the ability to see and understand how life works.

The Apostle Paul says:

> *"I pray the eyes of your heart may be enlightened in order that you may know the hope to which He has called you."* Ephesians 1:18

There is so much in the Bible about seeing spiritually, in other words, seeing and understanding spiritual truths and spiritual wisdom.

Clearly, light enables us to see. In the physical world, there are three things necessary in order to see. First, you need an object to look at, then, you must have the ability to see (your eyesight), and then, you must have light.

This is also true in the spiritual realm. You must have something to see, and that would be spiritual truth. You would need the ability to perceive this spiritual truth, and this is why we have a mind that can think, reason, and understand. Finally, you have light.

Jesus makes it clear that He is that light.

> John 1:9–*"This was the true Light that, coming into the world, enlightens every person."*

Jesus was the true light, and His teaching was light. He came to enlighten us. I find that one of the most exciting things in life is when God enlightens you to some new truth that will impact the way you see life, and the way you live your life.

In John 12:46 Jesus says: *"I have come as Light into the world, so that no one who believes in Me will remain in darkness."*

> In John 12:35–*So, Jesus said to them, "For a little while longer the Light is among you. Walk while you have the Light, so that darkness will not overtake you; also, the one who walks in the darkness does not know where he is going."*

The one verse in the Bible that reveals so much about Jesus being the light is:

John 8:12–*Then Jesus again spoke to them, saying, "I am the Light of the world; the one who follows Me will not walk in the darkness, but will have the Light of life."*

Jesus does not tell us He is a light in the world but that He is the light of the world and if we follow Him, we will not walk in the darkness. Why? Because in Him we will have *"the light of life."* That is a very strong statement that Christ is the light of life.

Tim Keller said this about light:

"The Bible sometimes compares God to the sun. The sun is a source of visual truth, because by it we see everything. And the sun is a source of biological life, because without it nothing could live. And God, the Bible says, is the source of all truth and all life. If you orbit around God, then your life has truth and vitality. You are in the light. But if you turn away from God and orbit around yourself, the result is spiritual darkness. You are turning away from the truth, away from life, toward darkness."

So, without Christ we walk in the darkness. What I have found to be true is that when a person lives in spiritual darkness, he thinks he is headed in the right direction, but he is lost. If you go back to John 12:35, Jesus says: *"he who walks in the darkness does not know where he goes."* When a person does not know where he is going, he is lost.

However, the good news according to the Apostle Peter is that when you become a Christian, God *"draws you out of darkness into His marvelous light."* (I Peter 2:9). This is truly good news.

NOTES:

THE PROMISES OF GOD

In the opening verses of II Peter, we learn:

II Peter 1:3,4–*"His divine power has given us everything we need for a godly life through our knowledge of Him who called us by his own glory and goodness. Through these he has given us His very great and precious promises, so that through them you may participate in the divine nature, having escaped the corruption in the world caused by evil desires."*

Here Peter refers to God's promises regarding our new life in Christ, especially the power of the Holy Spirit working in our lives. He refers to these promises as "great and precious" and through which we can experience His divine nature in us.

The Bible dictionary defines promises as "a declaration or assurance made to another person with respect to the future, stating that one will do or refrain from doing some specific thing, usually in a good sense implying something to the advantage or pleasure of the person concerned.

Promises give us assurance, stability, and hope as we face the future. Of course, a promise greatly depends on the reliability of the one who makes the promise. Is he trustworthy and is he capable of carrying it out? The writer of Hebrews says:

Hebrews 10:23 – *"Let's hold firmly to the confession of our hope without wavering, for He who promised is faithful."*

We are also told in Hebrews 6:19 that "...it is impossible for God to lie..."

I believe it is vitally important for us to understand how crucial promises are. For instance, Paul gives us some insight on why we should trust God because He is *"the God who raises the dead"* (II Corinthians 1:9) and for that reason, we put our faith and hope in Him.

Faith is ultimately putting our trust in what God has said and what He has promised. Doubting Thomas said he would not believe that Christ had risen unless he saw the imprint of the nails and could put his hand in Jesus' pierced side. When Jesus appears, and Thomas sees His wounds, he says, *"My Lord and my God."* And then Jesus responded, *"Because you have seen Me, have you believed? Blessed are they who did not see yet believed."* Jesus is talking about us. We have not seen what the disciples saw. We are left with God's

Word, His promises to us.

We see clearly how this worked out in the life of Abraham. Paul explains it in Romans 4:18-21.

> *"Against all hope, Abraham in hope believed and so became the father of many nations, just as it had been said to him, "So shall your offspring be." Without weakening in his faith, he faced the fact that his body was as good as dead—since he was about a hundred years old—and that Sarah's womb was also dead. Yet he did not waver through unbelief regarding the promise of God but was strengthened in his faith and gave glory to God, being fully persuaded that God had power to do what he had promised."*

Verse 20 gives us great insight into faith. Abraham based his faith on the promise of God that was revealed to him. Faith must have a foundation, and our foundation is the Old and New Testament which is His revealed Word.

One of the most powerful pictures of this is Jesus's words to His disciples just before He was crucified. They feared for their lives as Jesus has just told them He was leaving them. He gives them these words:

> John 14:1-3–*"Do not let your hearts be troubled. You believe in God; believe also in me. My Father's house has many rooms; if that were not so, would I have told you that I am going there to prepare a place for you? And if I go and prepare a place for you, I will come back and take you to be with me that you also may be where I am."*

Jesus is telling them that in the face of death, do not let your hearts be troubled. Why should their hearts not be troubled? He says because you should believe what I have told you. Believe My words. And then He tells them about there being many rooms in God's house. He then tells them they should believe it because "if it were not so I would have told you."

Faith is our responding to God's divine revelation. It is extending confidence in what God has said, revealed, and promised.

NOTES:

LESSON 33

SEEKING GOD'S GUIDANCE

I think it is vital to learn how to seek God's guidance as you walk through life, as you make decisions, as you seek God's will for your life.

It starts with the attitude of your heart. You must have the attitude of "wherever You lead me Lord, I will follow." A great approach is to tell Him: "Father I do not know what is best for my life, but you do." And then, go to the Scripture and pray for what He has committed to do.

> Psalm 31:3– *"For You are my rock and my fortress; For the sake of Your name, You will lead me and guide me."*

> Isaiah 48:17– *"This is what the LORD says—your Redeemer, the Holy One of Israel: "I am the LORD your God, who teaches you what is best for you, who directs you in the way you should go."*

> Psalm 32:8– *"I will instruct you and teach you in the way which you should go; I will counsel you with My eye upon you."*

And pray: "Lord, I stand on these promises as I look to You as my shepherd." I also pray Proverbs 16:3, from the New American Standard version, that says:

> *"Commit your works to the Lord and your plans will be established."*

The King James says:

> *"your thoughts will be established".*

The Amplified Bible says:

> *"Roll your works upon the Lord, commit and trust them wholly to Him; He will cause your thoughts to become agreeable to His will, and so shall your plans be established and succeed."*

A very wise man expounded on these verses with me and said we should ask God to establish our thinking and to work in our hearts and to incline our hearts to His will.

Solomon gives us some good instruction in:

> Proverbs 12:15– *"The way of a fool is right in his own eyes, But a person who listens to advice is wise."*

> Proverbs 15:22– *"Without consultation, plans are frustrated, But with many counselors they succeed."*

He makes it clear that it is good for us to seek wise counsel in making decisions.

I think it is natural to wonder how circumstances play a role in the decision-making process since God is sovereign over them. What I have found is that God generally uses circumstances to confirm or identify His leading.

We have to be very careful, for it is easy to use circumstances and our imagination to choose what we want to do.

Finally, I believe God confirms a decision by giving us a real peace as we make the decision. In fact, I suggest you pray: "Lord I pray that You will confirm the decision I am about to make by giving me a peace."

Then you must wait for His leading which is often the hard part.

> Isaiah 64:4–*"For from days of old they have not heard or perceived by ear, nor has the eye seen a God besides You, Who acts in behalf of one who waits for Him."*

It is imperative to remember that God, our Heavenly Father, promises to direct and guide the lives of His children. His timing is always perfect.

NOTES:

A LOVE OF THE TRUTH

I n the book of Jeremiah, you read of the rebelliousness and idolatry of God's people:

> Jeremiah 7:28–*"And you shall say to them, 'This is the nation that did not obey the voice of the Lord their God or accept discipline; truth has perished and has been eliminated from their mouth."*

The words that powerfully speak to me are "truth has perished." This reminds me of Paul's words to the church at Thessalonica. He speaks of *"those who perish because they did not receive the love of the truth so as to be saved."* (II Thessalonians 2:10). The Amplified Bible says, *"they refused to love the truth."*

The word truth is an important word that is used often in both the Old and New Testaments. So much of it refers to our relationship with the truth. Do we love the truth, and do we see it as our friend? I believe the healthiest people in life are those who love and follow the truth.

Jesus often refers to truth as light and falsehood as darkness. He has these powerful words to say in:

> John 3:19-21–*"This is the verdict: Light has come into the world, but people loved darkness instead of light because their deeds were evil. Everyone who does evil hates the light and will not come into the light for fear that their deeds will be exposed. But whoever lives by the truth comes into the light, so that it may be seen plainly that what they have done has been done in the sight of God."*

I find Jesus's words to Pontius Pilate about truth to be very enlightening. Jesus stands on trial before Pilate and Pilate asks Him, so you are a king? Jesus answered:

> John 18:37–*"You are right in saying, I am a king. In fact, for this reason I was born and for this I came into the world, to testify to the truth. Everyone on the side of truth hears My voice."*

Jesus is saying that if you do not love the truth, you will not hear His voice. I have concluded many people do not love the truth for they fear where it may take them.

George Graham, a retired philosophy professor who taught for a number of years at UAB said:

> "It takes a tremendous amount of courage to face the truth. People who have a habit of not facing the truth have a habit of having trouble living in every aspect of their lives – in their jobs, in their personal relationships; ... being centered on the truth is crucial to a healthy, vital human life."

It is important to realize God has called us to be truthful with ourselves, and that we be honest about our lives, our weaknesses, our fears, and our relationships.

There is some very significant teaching on this by Jesus in the Sermon of the Mount. We looked at this briefly in a prior lesson.

> Matthew 7:3-5–*"Why do you look at the speck that is in your brother's eye, but do not notice the log that is in your own eye? Or how can you say to your brother, 'Let me take the speck out of your eye,' and look, the log is in your own eye? You hypocrite, first take the log out of your own eye, and then you will see clearly to take the speck out of your brother's eye!"*

Jesus is teaching us that we so easily see flaws and weaknesses in the lives of others, but we can't see them in our own lives. We so easily concentrate our efforts on concealing our faults from others and even ourselves.

This is also a way to elevate ourselves and to feel better about ourselves. When I tear down someone else and point out their flaws and at the same time hide my own faults and pretend to be such a righteous, together person, I feel elevated and above others.

I believe it is crucial that we pray and ask God to show us the logs in our lives. We should also pray like David:

> Psalm 139:23, 24–*"Search me, God, and know my heart; Put me to the test and know my anxious thoughts; And see if there is any hurtful way in me and lead me in the everlasting way."*

> Psalm 26:2–*"Examine me, Lord, and put me to the test; Refine my [a] mind and my heart."*

In one sense, we are talking about seeing ourselves the way we really are, to see the truth about ourselves. For this to happen, God's word must be an integral part of my life. Listen to what Paul says:

> II Timothy 3:16–*"All Scripture is inspired by God and beneficial for teaching, for rebuke, for correction, for training in righteousness:"*

And in Hebrews 4:12 we are told that God's word is like a mirror

"that reveals the thoughts and intentions of our hearts."

As I said earlier, the healthiest people in life confront the truth about themselves and deal with the issues of life that must be dealt with, so that they can be authentic, real people whose lives are growing and being transformed.

This is also a key to the transformation of our relationships as it transforms the way we see others. For as Jesus clearly says, as we remove the logs from our lives, we will see others clearly, we will see them as God sees them. Not with a critical spirit, but with true compassion and love.

NOTES:

ONE OF LIFE'S MOST SIGNIFICANT PRINCIPLES

I remember several years ago my wife went to a seminar that was sponsored by a highly regarded woman counsellor. They were seeking to teach the participants how to help and minister to people in the midst of painful struggles in life. The foundation of their teaching and their understanding of peoples' problems is built upon this principle that I am going to share with you.

This principle comes from Paul's words in Galatians 6:7:

> *"Do not be deceived, God is not mocked; for whatever a person sows, this he will also reap."*

This is a common theme throughout the Bible.

In Isaiah 3:10 we are told we will :

> *"eat the fruit of our actions."*

In Jeremiah 17:10 God says:

> *"I give all people their due rewards, according to what their actions deserve."*

In Jeremiah 32:19 God:

> *"gives to everyone according to His ways according to the fruit of his deeds."*

Colossians 3:25:

> *"For the one who does wrong will receive the consequences of the wrong which he has done, and that without partiality."*

David gives us a picture of what is going on in this principle when he says in Psalm 7:17:

> *"He has dug a pit and hollowed it out and has fallen into the hole which he made."*

He says for many people life is like digging a hole and after digging it, he falls in the hole and struggles to get out.

I am not sure we grasp the magnitude of this teaching. In one sense God is not saying follow My ways or I will smack you. He is saying if you do not follow My ways, you will smack yourself. You will reap what you sow. So many people fail to realize that so many of our decisions and choices lead to an assault on our own beings.

Going back to Galatians 6:7, there are several significant words. He starts by saying,

> *"Do not be deceived." Clearly people are easily deceived into thinking I can make poor decisions for my life and get away with it, no consequences. God is making it clear; He will not be mocked. We are fools to believe we can live however we choose and not pay a price.*

I am reminded of the chilling words of author Oscar Wilde in his book, De Profundis: "Terrible as what the world did to me, what I did to myself was far more terrible still." This is why God asked the Israelites in Jeremiah 44:7:

> *"Why are you doing such great harm to yourselves?"*

There is one more key word in Galatians 6:7. It is the word "whatever." It is all inclusive. The law of sowing and reaping is functioning in every area of your life.

Every one of us is reaping financially from decisions we have made in the past. All of your relationships are reaping from what you have sown in the past. This includes your spiritual life, your career, your physical health, your intellect, and your morals. Whatever you sow, there will be a reaping.

Finally, we need to be reminded of Paul's words in Galatians 6:9.

> *"Let us not lose heart in making good choices, for over time we will reap if we do not grow weary and give up."*

Making choices is like planting seeds. The consequences are not immediate, but over time there will be a harvest, so do not lose heart, particularly if you are making good, wise choices.

NOTES:

THE VALUE OF WISDOM

W isdom is one of the most valuable possessions in all of life. Anyone can possess it, if they truly want it and if they are willing to seek and pursue it.

We learn from King Solomon of its incredible value in Proverbs 3:13-18.

> *"How blessed is the man who finds wisdom and the man who gains understanding." "For her profit is better than the profit of silver and her gain better than fine gold." "She is more precious than jewels; And nothing you desire compares with her." "Long life is in her right hand; In her left hand are riches and honor." "Her ways are pleasant ways, and her paths are peace."*
>
> *"She is a tree of life to those who take hold of her, and happy are all who hold her fast."*

I do not think many people really value wisdom for they do not know what it really is. The word "wisdom" comes from the Hebrew word chokmah that literally translates to have "skill or expertise in living." This essential component of wisdom gives one the ability to see things as they really are and not just as they appear to be. This ability is vital to the foundation of wisdom because we continually develop ideas explaining how our lives work as we move through various seasons of life. These ideas govern our thinking, designating what the world is like and how we are to live in it.

Scholar Neal Plantinga says wisdom is "finding out the truth about what life is, what makes the world work and how we ought to fit into it." This explains why wisdom is of such great value. It not only gives coherence to life but provides a path leading to our ultimate well-being and happiness. We should all stop and ask, "What is that worth to me?"

I would like to share three thoughts on obtaining wisdom. First, in Proverbs 9:10 we are told:

> *"The fear of the Lord is the beginning of wisdom."*

Most believe this means to respect and revere the Lord, which is true. However, we are to fear God's Word. He deals with us according to His Word. We should ultimately fear the consequences of departing from His Word, for this is where wisdom begins.

Second, we are told to ask God to give us wisdom. In James 1:5 we are told:

"If any of you lacks wisdom, you should ask God, who gives generously to all without finding fault, and it will be given to you."

If this is true, we should be asking for God's wisdom every day. In fact, we should ask for wisdom regarding specific issues, like "Lord I pray that you would give me wisdom to better love my spouse."

Finally, it is crucial to know and understand what Paul tell us in Colossians 2:3: *"that in Christ are hidden all the treasures of wisdom and knowledge."* He is the source.

Therefore, when a person enters into a relationship with Him and gets to know and love Him, that person will become wise. Christ is the ultimate guide in life, and it is therefore critical that we stay close to Him and walk through life with Him.

NOTES:

THE SIGNIFICANCE OF BIBLICAL PROPHECY

A s the years have gone by, I have learned of the great importance of Biblical prophecy. It is a great demonstration of the power of God. The fulfillment of the Messianic prophesies has led many Jewish people to become Christians as they conclude Jesus is their Messiah.

In the Bible, prophecy is a message from God about the future. We receive good insight into prophecy in the book of Isaiah 46:10

> *"Declaring the end from the beginning, and from ancient times things which have not been done, saying, 'My plan will be established, And I will accomplish all My good pleasure.'"*

When Jesus had risen from the dead and was meeting the disciples for the very last time, He shared with them all the prophecies in the Old Testament that foretold of His coming. Luke 24:44-47:

> *"He said to them, "These are my words that I spoke to you while I was still with you, that everything written about me in the law of Moses and in the prophets and psalms must be fulfilled." Then he opened their minds to understand the scriptures. And he said to them, "Thus it is written that the Messiah would suffer and rise from the dead on the third day and that repentance, for the forgiveness of sins, would be preached in his name to all the nations, beginning from Jerusalem."*

Then we see how the disciples went out into the world and in proclaiming the gospel message would demonstrate from the Old Testament how Jesus had in fact fulfilled the prophecies of the coming Messiah.

Acts 17:1-4:

> *"When they took the road through Amphipolis and Apollonia, they reached Thessalonica, where there was a synagogue of the Jews. Following his usual custom, Paul joined them, and for three sabbaths he entered into discussions with them from the scriptures, expounding and demonstrating that the Messiah had to suffer and rise from the dead, and that "This is the Messiah, Jesus, whom I proclaim to you." Some of them were convinced and joined Paul and Silas; so, too, a great number of Greeks who were worshipers, and not a few of the*

prominent women."

Most of us are familiar with several of the prophecies that are generally read in the Christmas season regarding the birth of the coming Messiah.

• He will be born in Bethlehem. Micah 5:2

> *"But you, Bethlehem Ephrathah, though you are small among the clans of Judah, out of you will come for me one who will be ruler over Israel, whose origins are from of old, from ancient times."*

• He will be born of a virgin. Isaiah 7:14

> *"Therefore, the Lord Himself will give you a sign: Behold, the virgin will conceive and give birth to a son, and she will name Him Immanuel."*

I think my favorite among all of these is Isaiah 9:6.

> *"For a Child will be born to us, a Son will be given to us;*
> *And the government will rest on His shoulders;*
> *And His name will be called Wonderful Counselor, Mighty God,*
> *Eternal Father, Prince of Peace."*

This is very powerful. A son will be born to us, and He will be called "Mighty God." God in the flesh as a person. It is also important to note that Isaiah penned these words 700 years before Christ was born.

Finally, the most powerful of all the Messianic prophecies I believe is found in the 53rd chapter of Isaiah. It is a picture of a suffering servant:

v. 4-5 He bore our suffering.

> *"Surely, he took up our pain and bore our suffering, yet we considered him punished by God, stricken by him, and afflicted. But he was pierced for our transgressions, he was crushed for our iniquities; the punishment that brought us peace was on him, and by his wounds we are healed."*

v. 6 He defines sin as wanting to go my own way. He caused my iniquity, my sin to fall on this suffering servant so it would not have to fall on me.

> *"We all, like sheep, have gone astray, each of us has turned to our own way; and the Lord has laid on him the iniquity of us all."*

v. 7 He did not open His mouth.

> *"He was oppressed and afflicted, yet he did not open his mouth; he was led like a lamb to the slaughter, and as a sheep before its shearers is silent, so he did not open his mouth."*

v. 9 He was crucified between two criminals but was buried by Joseph of Arimathea, a wealthy man.

> *"He was assigned a grave with the wicked, and with the rich in his death, though he had done no violence, nor was any deceit in his mouth."*

v. 10 God was pleased to do this for us, because of His great love for us.

> *"Yet it was the Lord's will to crush him and cause him to suffer, and though the Lord makes his life an offering for sin, he will see his offspring and prolong his days, and the will of the Lord will prosper in his hand."*

v. 12 He bore the sin of many.

> *"Therefore, I will give him a portion among the great, and he will divide the spoils with the strong, because he poured out his life unto death, and was numbered with the transgressors. For he bore the sin of many and made intercession for the transgressors."*

This is powerful evidence that Jesus was the long-awaited Jewish Messiah.

NOTES:

BEING EMOTIONALLY HEALTHY

H ans Selye was a scientist from Canada who was a true pioneer in discovering the impact of emotions on a person's health, writing more than 30 books on the subject.

In his landmark publication, *The Stress of Life*, Selye's research uncovered a principle that is crucial for a person to have if they are to be emotionally healthy. Creating a fancy term for it, he named it altruistic egoism.

As complex as that may sound, it is nothing more than the Biblical truth—"helping others helps you."

In Luke 6:38, Jesus says, *"Give and it will be given unto you."* In Proverbs we are told: *"A generous man will prosper; he who refreshes others will himself be refreshed."* In other words, when we enrich someone else's life, we find our own lives enriched. Seyle observed this principle at work during years and years of research.

This principle in its simplest form states, "We receive in this life by giving." God designed the human heart to give, and we receive great joy in this life when we give.

This may sound self-serving to some, that I should give to others so that I can receive. But, in reality, God is telling us this is the way I designed you. This is the way you will function best as a human being.

So, if this is true, then the inverse of this principle is also true, that self-centeredness leads to misery in life. I would also add that self-centeredness is what leads to certain mental health problems.

Several years ago, an interesting book was published, selling thousands of copies. *The Narcissism Epidemic* was written by two American psychologists and focused on the significant shift that has occurred in our culture's psychology: the relentless rise of narcissism.

Narcissism is defined as "an excessive interest in oneself and one's physical appearance." The authors contend that this epidemic of narcissism has resulted in people being more depressed, more discontented, and more unhappy than ever before.

When we fail to do what God designed us to do, it is just a matter of time before we malfunction.

In Romans 15:1 Paul tells us that "those who are healthy and have strength should seek to bear the weaknesses of those without strength and not just live to please ourselves. The heart of selfishness is the desire to live for yourself and to please yourself without any regard for other people.

Paul goes on to share a similar thought in Philippians 2:3, 4:

> *"Do nothing from selfishness or empty conceit, but with humility consider one another as more important than yourselves; do not merely look out for your own personal interests, but also for the interests of others."*

> I Corinthians 10:24–*"Don't be concerned for your own good but for the good of others."*

> I Thessalonians 5:15–*"...always seek after that which is good for one another and for all people."*

> James 3:16–*"For whenever there is jealousy and selfish ambition, there you will find disorder and evil of every kind."*

> Mark 12:31–*"You shall love your neighbor as yourself."*

The story is told by Dr. M. Scott Peck, the famous psychologist and author, who describes a woman patient who suffered from extreme depression. One day, when she was scheduled for an appointment, she called and told Dr. Peck her car had broken down. He offered to pick her up on his way to work, but explained he had to make a hospital call before he got to the office. If she was willing to wait in the car while he made the call, they could have their appointment. She agreed.

When they got to the hospital, he had another suggestion. He gave her the names of two of his patients who were convalescing there and told her that each of them would enjoy a visit from her. When they met again an hour and a half later, the woman was on an emotional high. She told Dr. Peck that trying to cheer up the patients had lifted her spirits, causing her to feel incredible.

Dr. Peck responded by saying, "Well, now we know how to get you out of your depression. We know the cure for your problem."

The woman answered, "You don't expect me to do that every day, do you?"

When you enrich someone else's life, you find your own life enriched. However, when one is consumed with themselves, it is just a matter of time before they find themselves depleted and emotionally impoverished.

NOTES:

LESSON 39

GOD'S OBJECTIVE FOR THE CHRISTIAN LIFE

PART I

A number of years ago I read an article in the newspaper that I have never forgotten. I am not sure where the journalist got his information, but I think he was probably on target. He said that only 5% of the population has a clearly defined strategy for their lives. The other 95% live reactively. Their lives are nothing more than a response to what happens to them. They have no plan to make life conform to their dreams, their goals, their mission in life.

I share this because this has real application to the spiritual realm and our spiritual lives. What objectives does God have for me, for my life as a Christian? I find it is so easy for us as followers of Christ to spiritually drift through life with no objective to where we are going.

I believe God's ultimate objective for a Christian is embodied in some of Christ's most significant words, in fact these are some of His last words here on earth:

> Matthew 28:18-20– *"And Jesus came up and spoke to them, saying, "All authority in heaven and on earth has been given to Me. Go, therefore, and make disciples of all the nations, baptizing them in the name of the Father and the Son and the Holy Spirit, teaching them to follow all that I commanded you; and behold, am with you always, to the end of the age."*

This was Jesus' instruction to the disciples and to the early church. Notice He does not say go out and make a bunch of Christians converts. He is very clear that we are to go out into the world and make disciples.

The word disciple comes from a Latin root which means learner or pupil.

> Luke 6:17– *"And then Jesus came down with them and stood on a level place; and there was a large crowd of His disciples, and a great multitude of the people from all Judea and Jerusalem, and the coastal region of Tyre and Sidon."*

In the New Testament, we read of Jesus's twelve disciples, but you had scores of Christians, but as this verse indicates, "there was a multitude of disciples." This was the designation given to Christians who were following Him and seeking to carry out His work in the world. To play a role in the process.

This is what the celebrated philosopher Dallas Willard said about discipleship:

"A disciple is a learner, a student, an apprentice—a practitioner, even if only a beginner. The New Testament literature, which must be allowed to define our terms if we are ever to get our bearings in the Way with Christ, makes this clear. In that context, disciples of Jesus are people who do not just profess certain views as their own but apply their growing understanding of life in the Kingdom of the Heavens to every aspect of their life on earth."

Willard is telling us my relationship with God should impact who I am as a person. It should impact you as a spouse, a parent, your business life, and your social public life. Willard goes on the say:

"The disciple stands as an envoy or a receiver by which the kingdom of God is conveyed into every quarter of human affairs."

So, our relationship with Christ should make a real difference in our lives. The big question is, how does one become a disciple? Well, it comes the same way you become a doctor, lawyer, accountant, or mechanic. You have to be trained and equipped. Then you have to put into practice what you have learned.

Think about Jesus' disciples, they spent three years under His teaching. When Paul became a Christian, he did not rush off to change the world. In Galatians 1:16, Paul says he did not rush out "to consult with any man, nor did I go to Jerusalem to meet with the Apostles."

He went away for three years for training. First in Arabia and then back to Damascus. It was only then that he met with Peter and the other Apostles.

Paul then speaks to the same training for Christians in the church.

> Ephesians 4:11,12–*"So Christ himself gave the apostles, the prophets, the evangelists, the pastors and teachers, to equip his people for works of service, so that the body of Christ may be built up."*

This is the way the church is supposed to function. We think erroneously that pastors, teachers, and evangelists are to do the work of service and build up the body of Christ, and we sit on the sidelines and watch.

Think about the equipping and training process. When you equip someone, you train them so they can take on a responsibility. That is true in any field. Paul tells us of this responsibility we are being trained to do. Go back to

Ephesians 4:12:

> *"...to prepare God's people for works of service, so that the body of Christ might be built up."*

God's desire is that we grow spiritually and be fully trained and equipped as Christ's disciples. When we are, it impacts the type of person I become, and it impacts what I do with my life.

NOTES:

GOD'S OBJECTIVE FOR THE CHRISTIAN LIFE

PART II

I would like to start this lesson with two good insights into discipleship: R. C. Sproul–

"The New Testament word for disciple means literally a 'learner.' A disciple does not dabble in learning but makes the seeking after an understanding of God—a chief business of his life."

I think one of the reasons so many modern Christians fail to make this the chief end of life is because we easily become passionate about things that simply do no matter.

Dallas Willard –

"...the greatest issue facing the world today, with all its heartbreaking needs is whether those who, by profession or culture, are identified as 'Christians' will become disciples – students, apprentices, practitioners of Jesus Christ, steadily learning from Him how to live the (Christian life and take it) into every corner of human existence."

I would now like to point you back to a verse that reveals a great deal about being a disciple of Christ. It is in the book of John where Jesus teaches about the vine/branch relationship. So much of this teaching is about bearing fruit and then Jesus says in verse 8 (of Chapter 15).

> *"By this is my Father glorified, that you bear much fruit and so prove to be My disciple."*

A disciple of Christ bears fruit. In fact, as you read both the Old and New Testaments, it strikes me very powerfully God's expectation that His people be fruitful. It does not seem to be an option. He expects us to be productive and, as Paul says in Romans 7:4, *"...bear fruit for God."*

A very wise man shared with me that we were designed to be spiritually productive, and if we are not, we will experience a great deal of spiritual frustration.

Jesus tells several parables about a wealthy man who goes off on a journey to a distant land. Before leaving, he allots to the slaves who work for him a certain amount of money. He instructed them to be productive with the money he entrusted them with. In these parables, the master of these slaves eventually returns and asks each of these men to give an account. He gives great praise and reward to those who were productive and fruitful. He lashes out and even punishes those who bore no fruit.

You see this expectation for fruit in the Old Testament as well. It comes in a song in Isaiah 5:1-6:

> *"I will sing for the one I love*
> *a song about his vineyard:*
> *My loved one had a vineyard*
> *on a fertile hillside.*
> *He dug it up and cleared it of stones*
> *and planted it with the choicest vines.*
> *He built a watchtower in it*
> *and cut out a winepress as well.*
> *Then he looked for a crop of good grapes,*
> *but it yielded only bad fruit.*
> *"Now you dwellers in Jerusalem and people of Judah,*
> *judge between me and my vineyard.*
> *What more could have been done for my vineyard*
> *than I have done for it?*
> *When I looked for good grapes,*
> *why did it yield only bad?*
> *Now I will tell you*
> *what I am going to do to my vineyard:*
> *I will take away its hedge,*
> *and it will be destroyed;*
> *I will break down its wall,*
> *and it will be trampled.*
> *I will make it a wasteland,*
> *neither pruned nor cultivated,*
> *and briers and thorns will grow there.*
> *I will command the clouds*
> *not to rain on it."*

What strikes me is that the owner of the vineyard (who represents God), made everything available to assist in the fertility of the vine. Consequently, there was no excuse for not bearing fruit. How did the owner respond? He was angry. He expected to find fruit, and there was no excuse for not bearing fruit.

So, what does it specifically mean to be fruitful? Webster's says, "fruit is the end product of plant growth." So, spiritual fruit is the end product of spiritual growth.

In the Bible, there are two components of bearing fruit. First, think in terms of fruit generated by a tree. The fruit distinguishes it from all other trees. It is the visible manifestation of the tree's end product. If we are growing spiritually, there should be some type of manifestation of this growth. There should be a changed life, there should be fruit that the world can see.

In Galatians, Paul gives us a description of this fruit.

> Galatians 5:22,23–*"But the fruit of the Spirit is love, joy, peace, forbearance, kindness, goodness, faithfulness, gentleness and self-control. Against such things there is no law."*

Notice Paul describes it as "the fruit of the spirit." It is the visible manifestation of God's spirit working in our lives. It is the result of abiding and walking in the power of the Holy Spirit which we discussed in Lessons 36 and 37.

The second component of fruit we read about in Philippians 1:22 where Paul speaks of "fruitful labor" in the lives of others. Jesus addresses this also.

> John 4:34-38–*"Jesus said to them, "My food is to do the will of Him who sent Me, and to accomplish His work. Do you not say, 'There are still four months, and then comes the harvest'? Behold, I tell you, raise your eyes and observe the fields, that they are white for harvest. Already the one who reaps is receiving wages and is gathering fruit for eternal life, so that the one who sows and the one who reaps may rejoice together. For in this case the saying is true: 'One sows, and another reaps.' I sent you to reap that for which you have not labored; others have labored, and you have come into their labor."*

Jesus uses the words harvest and reaping. These words refer to the disciple making process.

It is to help people find Christ and then equip them to be disciples. Isn't this what Jesus instructed the early church to do?

> *"Go therefore and make disciples..."*

Jesus also points out a problem that was present during His time and is also a problem today.

> Matthew 9:37,38–*"Then He said to His disciples, "The harvest is plentiful, but the workers are few. Therefore, plead with the Lord of the harvest to send out workers into His harvest."*

We need more laborers in the harvest, let's be praying that God will raise them up.

Finally, keep these words of Jesus ever before you:

> *"By this is My Father glorified that you bear much fruit and so prove to be My disciple." John 15:5*

NOTES:

SPEAKING PROGRAMS WITH THE AUTHOR

Richard E. Simmons III welcomes inquiries and is available for
speaking opportunities to groups, meetings, and conferences.

For information on scheduling contact:
Kim Knott at
kim@thecenterbham.org

ALSO BY RICHARD E. SIMMONS III

All books are available from our website:
richardesimmons3.com

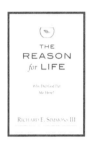

THE REASON FOR LIFE

Why Did God Put Me Here?

Why was I born? Why am I living? In this book I seek to answer
these questions recognising that if there is a God out there, why did
he put me here? What is the reason for my earthly existance? I hope
the insight in this book might enable you to understand what is the
reason for life.

A LIFE OF EXCELLENCE—GRADUATION EDITION

Wisdom for Effective Living

For the graduate in your life. *A Life of Excellence* lays out three
principles that clearly point to a life of excellence. I am convinced that
if one lives in accordance with these principles, their life will flourish
and prosper.

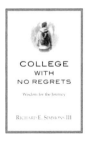

COLLEGE WITH NO REGRETS

Wisdom for the Journey

College is one of the most exciting and meaningful times in life.
However, for all the exciting things college offers, it may bring
big questions—perhaps even some fear or anxiety. This book will
make you wiser and equip you to better navigate your own journey
through the college experience.

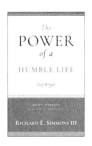

THE POWER OF A HUMBLE LIFE

Quiet Strength in an Age of Arrogance

This book examines what I consider to be life's greatest paradox—that
strength is found in humility.

WISDOM: LIFE'S GREAT TREASURE

Timeless Essays on the Art of Intentional Living

A collection of short essays on wisdom to serve as a guide to help people walk in wisdom on their journey towards a healthy and meaningful life.

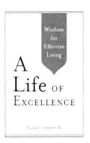

A LIFE OF EXCELLENCE

Wisdom for Effective Living

A Life of Excellence lays out three principles that clearly point to a life of excellence. I am convinced that if one lives in accordance with these principles, their life will flourish and prosper.

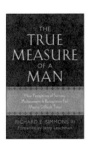

THE TRUE MEASURE OF A MAN

How Perceptions of Success, Achievement & Recognition Fail Men in Difficult Times

In our performance-driven culture this book provides liberating truth on how to be set free from fear of failure, comparing ourselves to others and the false ideas we have about masculinity.

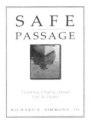

SAFE PASSAGE

Thinking Clearly about Life & Death

Safe Passage examines C. S. Lewis's thoughts and perspective on the issue of human mortality.

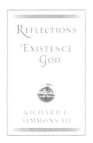

REFLECTIONS ON THE EXISTENCE OF GOD

A Series of Essays

This book is a series of short essays seeking to answer life's most enduring question: Does God exist? I have attempted to craft a book that is well researched but also easy to read and understand. Each essay can be read in less that 10 minutes. In the end it is important to know whether God exists or He does not exist. There is no third option. What I am Seeking to do in this book is to determine which of these beliefs is true and which one is not.

RELIABLE TRUTH

The Validity of the Bible in an Age of Skepticism

Do you believe the Bible is the inspired word of God? *Reliable Truth* offers powerful and compelling evidence why the Bible is valid and true.

REMEMBERING THE FORGOTTEN GOD

The Search for Truth in the Modern World

A fresh, contemporary approach to Christianity, a compassionate yet forceful statement of personal belief.

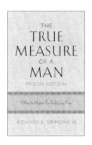

THE TRUE MEASURE OF A MAN—PRISON EDITION

How Perceptions of Success, Achievement &Recognition Fail Men in Difficult Times

In our performance-driven culture this book provides liberating truth on how to be set free from fear of failure, comparing ourselves to others and the false ideas we have about masculinity.

SEX AT FIRST SIGHT

Understanding the Modern HookupCulture

This book explains the Hookup culture—how it came about, how it is affecting our younger generation and finally, God's intent for our sexuality.